Spiritual Challenge Journal

the NEXT LEVEL

WWJD

A disciple's 30-day adventure in following Jesus, for
students who want to be more than just religious

D1307517

More student journals for you from Youth Specialties!

WWJD Spiritual Challenge Journal
Wild Truth Journal for Junior Highers
Grow For It Journal through the Scriptures
Grow For It Journal

Spiritual Challenge Journal

the NEXT LEVEL

WWJD

A disciple's
30-day
adventure in
following
Jesus, for
students who
want to be
more than just
religious

Mike Yaconelli

Youth Specialties

ZondervanPublishingHouse
Grand Rapids, Michigan
A Division of HarperCollinsPublishers

WWJD Spiritual Challenge Journal—The Next Level: A disciple's 30-day adventure in following Jesus, for students who want to be more than just religious

©1999 by Youth Specialties, Inc.

Youth Specialties Books, 1224 Greenfield Dr., El Cajon, CA 92021, are published by Zondervan Publishing House, 5300 Patterson Ave. S.E., Grand Rapids, MI 49530.

Unless otherwise indicated, all Scripture quotations are taken from the *Holy Bible: New International Version* (North American Edition). Copyright ©1973, 1978, 1984 by International Bible Society. Used by permission of Zondervan Publishing House.

WWJD logo used by permission of ForeFront Records.

Edited by Randy Southern and Tim McLaughlin
Cover and interior design by Patton Brothers Design

Printed in the United States of America

ISBN 0-310-22985-5

99 00 01 02 03/ /10 9 8 7 6 5 4 3 2

CONTENTS

The NEXT Level Adventure

Day 15	Human
Day 16	Hungry
Day 17	Immature
Day 18	Incapable
Day 19	Independent
Day 20	Mature
Day 21	Ordinary
Day 22	Overconfident
Day 23	Practical
Day 24	Prepared
Day 25	Seeking
Day 26	Sensitive
Day 27	Servant-like
Day 28	Shrewd
Day 29	Strong
Day 30	Weak

DISCIPLE—whoa, now *there's* a fun word.

Sounds like something most any dork would like to be.

"What I'd really like to be when I grow up is a disciple." Yeah, right.

The youth workers in my church use that word a lot. They're always asking, "Do you want to be discipled?" or "Don't you want to be in a discipleship group?"

Oh, yeah. I'm there.

First of all, how can I be discipled when I don't even know what a disciple is? I mean, I know that Jesus had these disciple guys who followed him around all the time. And I know they were these super-religious guys who hung out with Jesus and helped him—like when blind people couldn't find Jesus or when those dudes with the spooky skin disease came to him.

I think the disciples may have been Jesus' bodyguards, too. They tried to keep him from all these strange people, except Jesus would yell at them and actually let the strange people come to him.

I know the disciples were very cool religious dudes—except for the narc, the Judas guy, who finally ratted on Jesus. That's right, isn't it? I mean, the disciples were really dedicated to Jesus, weren't they? So I guess when my youth worker wants to "disciple" me, he wants me to be *really* religious, *really* Christian. You know, read the Bible, pray, go to church all the time, tell everyone I can about Jesus.

That's what a disciple does, right?

At least that's what I *used* to think. Until I read

the Bible, especially the New Testament. I was blown away when I took the time to read about the real disciples. Those dudes were clueless. I'm not kidding. They were always screwing up.

Most of the time when the disciples speak in the Bible, they're asking Jesus a question. And when he answers the question, they *still* don't know what he's talking about. No matter what Jesus taught, the disciples didn't understand it. When Jesus said he was going to die, they didn't believe him. Just before Jesus was arrested, he asked the disciples to stay up late and pray with him—and they fell asleep. When a group of children rushed up affectionately to Jesus, the disciples tried to herd them away ("Don't bother this Very Important Man"), only to be reprimanded by the Master. The kids loved Jesus, and Jesus loved to hang around the kids. (Wouldn't you, if most of the adults in your life either didn't understand you or wanted to kill you?) And when Jesus died, the disciples figured everything was over and went back to their old lives. Until Jesus showed up again, that is.

I realized that if disciples were that messed up and still disciples, then it was possible for me to become one. If Jesus called that erratic, unstable, bewildered, inconsistent, and questioning group of disciples to follow him...well, just maybe he would call me.

Despite what happened to the disciples when they were with Jesus, history tells us that all of them (except Judas) became fearless followers of Jesus. So, I concluded, disciples are apparently screwed-up people who are willing to follow Jesus, messed-up people whom Jesus likes anyway.

For the next 30 days you're going to have the adventure of your life—just like the disciples did. They never knew what was going to happen from one day to the next...didn't have a clue what would be demanded of them every minute...no idea that following Jesus would make the rest of their lives a roller coaster of adventure, fear, intensity, exhilaration, doubt, sadness, laughter, passion, loss, deep friendships, terror, love, betrayal, and gratitude. It didn't seem to matter that being a disciple of Jesus eventually cost most of them their lives. What *did* matter most to them was that never in their wildest dreams could they have known an adventure like the one they lived.

If you could talk to Jesus' disciples now, I think, one by one, they'd say, "What a ride!" That's the kind of life I'm looking for. And it sounds like I'm the kind of person Jesus is looking for.

So check out this discipleship thing. Maybe you have nothing to lose...maybe you have *everything* to lose. Maybe losing everything allows you to live the real thing.

And maybe being a disciple isn't a bad way to go. Maybe it's the only way. ◆

AFRAID

Disciple Story

Mark 4:35-41

That day when evening came, he said to his disciples, "Let us go over to the other side." Leaving the crowd behind, they took him along, just as he was, in the boat. There were also other boats with him. A furious squall came up, and the waves broke over the boat, so that it was nearly swamped. Jesus was in the stern, sleeping on a cushion. The disciples woke him and said to him, "Teacher, don't you care if we drown?"

He got up, rebuked the wind and said to the waves, "Quiet! Be still!" Then the wind died down and it was completely calm.

He said to his disciples, "Why are you afraid? Do you still have no faith?"

They were terrified and asked each other, "Who is this? Even the wind and the waves obey him!"

Afraid can suggest weakness or cowardice. Other times, though, being afraid is a *good* thing. There's a fine line between fear that comes from weakness and fear that respects strength. It's okay, for example, to be afraid of tornadoes or hurricanes or earthquakes—or even a "furious squall."

When his fearful disciples came to him in the middle of the storm, Jesus asked them to think about why they were afraid. As the disciples demonstrated, the best thing to do with a healthy fear is to take that fear to the Lord. You can bet that whatever causes you to be afraid doesn't cause Jesus to be afraid—and *that* ought to make you afraid. Think about it—being afraid is good when it activates all your senses, causes you to be cautious, gets your adrenalin pumping, and prepares you to respond to danger.

Being afraid is also good when it causes you to recognize how big, powerful, and awesome God is. When disciples are afraid of God, it's because they respect him. The disciples were afraid of Jesus many times—and that's what made them good disciples.

Disciple Dilemma

Life is hard in what's left of Cheryl's family. She's a city girl whose single mom has no time to take her camping or hiking in the mountains. In fact, her mom has no time for hardly anything except working. She seems to work all the time, and Cheryl has to work weekends to help out. It's not exactly a *bad* life, but it's hard—not much money, not much free time, not many relationships, no vacations, and no time to herself. Cheryl hasn't seen her dad in five years. Frankly, though, she has no desire to see him or communicate with him. Cheryl feels distant from most people. She doesn't really have time for relationships, but then most of the guys she knows are clueless about responsibility and commitment.

The bright light in Cheryl's life is church. Her mom makes sure they both have time for church. And youth group, which Cheryl looks forward to every week—and not just for the spiritual growth. For Cheryl youth group is a wonderful distraction from her everyday routine.

Last week was the most amazing experience Cheryl ever had. Somehow she and her mom had saved enough money for Cheryl to go to the church summer retreat. Cheryl had never been to a camp before, not to mention the mountains. One night she snuck out of her cabin to sleep under the stars. She had never seen so many stars, never seen such beauty. As Cheryl stared at the sky, she felt a strange surge of emotion. Her eyes filled with tears as she realized for the first time just how huge the universe is,

how magnificent God's creation is, and how tiny she is. She had heard about God's love since she was a little kid in Sunday school, but somehow his bigness and her tininess—and his love for her—seemed overwhelming. Cheryl began crying.

It was then she became afraid. *What's the matter with me?* she thought. *Am I losing it? God is much bigger than I ever imagined and I am just a nobody, a nothing. Why should this God care about me? What if I mess up? What will happen to me if I really give my life to a God this big? Why do I feel so scared?*

Cheryl fell asleep crying. Camp ended the next day, but Cheryl still hasn't recovered. She is afraid to talk to anyone about her experience. She is beginning to wonder if something is wrong with her.

The Obvious
The disciples were afraid even though Jesus was with them.
[When was the last time you were afraid?]

The Lesson
Fear is not all bad if it drives you to Jesus.
[It's one thing when Jesus is in your boat and you can physically touch him, but what about here and now? How do you bring your fear to Jesus now?]

The Not-So-Obvious
The disciples were more afraid after Jesus calmed the storm.
[Ever had a moment when you were afraid of God?]

The Not-So-Obvious Lesson
Sometimes the problem of a storm is only replaced by the problem of Jesus.
[How would you put the Not-So-Obvious Lesson in your own words?]

for your write hand

• What did Cheryl's experience teach you about being a disciple?

Nothing really

• What would Jesus say to you right now about being afraid?

Dont be afraid of what you dont know about.

exit poll

"Jesus was ticked off at the disciples for being afraid. Christians are not supposed to be wimps. If you are afraid of anything as a Christian there is something wrong with you. How can you be afraid when you have Jesus in your heart?"

ALIENS

Disciple story

1 Peter 2:9-12

But you are a chosen people, a royal priesthood, a holy nation, a people belonging to God, that you may declare the praises of him who called you out of darkness into his wonderful light. Once you were not a people, but now you are the people of God; once you had not received mercy, but now you have received mercy.

Dear friends, I urge you, as aliens and strangers in the world, to abstain from sinful desires, which war against your soul. Live such good lives among the pagans that, though they accuse you of doing wrong, they may see your good deeds and glorify God on the day he visits us.

Aliens are foreigners, strangers in a strange land. Aliens don't speak the native language, don't follow the customs and traditions, don't fit in. Aliens are typically uncomfortable, awkward, unsure of themselves in their new—though foreign—home.

Disciples are aliens in this world. Many of our culture's values are foreign to a disciple. Disciples don't naturally fit into a society that is largely out of touch with God. They are uncomfortable, looking and feeling out of place in the everyday world. Disciples of Christ find themselves continually at odds with the culture, because they have different values, different priorities, a different language. Disciples feel odd and estranged in modern culture—and that's just how they ought to feel.

Disciple Dilemma

Diane (everyone called her "Lady Di" because she looked just like the late Princess of Wales) found herself at the center of the conversation. The slumber party had been going strong since last night and now, at three in the morning, the talk was getting serious.

"Come on, Diane, what do you mean you've never looked at a Victoria's Secret catalog? It's more than the underwear—which, frankly, I can't believe you don't care about. It's the *models*. They look so good. I want to know their secret—don't you?"

"Not really," Di said. "That's why I don't go out with guys right now. I'm too young, too easily influenced by guys. I could easily be obsessed with how I look. And I know this sounds stupid, but my faith really matters to me. Thinking about guys and about my body and my clothes and my makeup all the time doesn't make a lot of sense when I put God in the picture."

"Get *real*, Di. The only reason you're saying that is because you already have a body worth dying for and looks to go with it. Every guy in class wants to go out with you. I mean, come on, you want to learn more about God? That's psycho. What's wrong with you?"

Diane sat up, not sure if it was anger or hurt feelings that she felt inside.

"Hey, I know, I know. Girls are considered crazy if they don't sit around drooling over guys and trying to turn them on by wearing tight skirts and miracle bras. Frankly, I don't like being pretty because it keeps people from trying to get to know me. I think it's sick to turn on guys just so I can feel good. Besides, I don't want some horny guy who just likes my body. Call me weird if you want, but I am totally happy to have no guys in my life right now."

The conversation ended awkwardly and Diane eventually fell asleep. Later on that night something woke her up, and she'd rather not have heard the whispered conversation.

"...but she doesn't make sense. She's full of crap and you know it. Either Diane's lying or she's a lesbian—and I wouldn't be surprised if she was a lesbian. She's just plain weird. All this talk about God is a bunch of baloney." Diane pretended to turn over in her sleep so no one could see her crying.

The Obvious

Disciples should feel uncomfortable with the values of their culture.

[What values do you feel uncomfortable with?]

The Lesson

The closer you get to Jesus, the more alien you will be to the culture.

[How would the Lesson sound in your own words?]

The Not-So-Obvious

Living an alien life can also attract people to Jesus.

[Have any friends you hope are attracted to your alien lifestyle? Who are they?]

The Not-So-Obvious Lesson

Disciples focus on Jesus, not on whether people are responding positively or negatively to them.

[How can you focus on Jesus?]

for your write hand

• What did Diane's experience at the slumber party teach you about being a disciple?

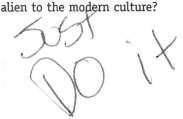

It sucks

• What would Jesus say to you right now about being alien to the modern culture?

Just Do it

exit poll

"Sometimes I think Christians want the rest of us to think they are fruitcakes. I mean, I had this friend invite me to his church and the next thing I know everyone is on their feet dancing around like idiots. Even my buddy is raising his hands in the air and getting all bizarre. Then he looks at me and says, 'Isn't this cool? Wouldn't you like to be happy like everyone here?' I'm thinking, 'Oh, yeah, I want to be like all you bimbos.' All I could think about was getting the heck out of there. I mean, give me a break, they say they don't mind being persecuted because that's what happens when you follow Jesus. Ha! Jesus didn't act like a dork. He told people the truth and tried to help people. He didn't just make a spectacle of himself. Like I say, my friend and his church don't want me to know about Jesus, they want me to join a bunch of crazies. Sorry. Not for me."

✗

AUTHORITY

Mark 2:23-28

One Sabbath Jesus was going through the grainfields, and as his disciples walked along, they began to pick some heads of grain. The Pharisees said to him, "Look, why are they doing what is unlawful on the Sabbath?"

He answered, "Have you never read what David did when he and his companions were hungry and in need? In the days of Abiathar the high priest, he entered the house of God and ate the consecrated bread, which is lawful only for priests to eat. And he also gave some to his companions."

Then he said to them, "The Sabbath was made for man, not man for the Sabbath. So the Son of Man is Lord even of the Sabbath."

Authority is a word that most young people don't use for one simple reason: it's a power word, and adults are the ones who generally have it all. When adults want to describe reachable goals for you, they usually use words like *maturity*, *growth*, *humility*, or *patience*. But seldom if ever *authority*.

But disciples of Jesus can have authority whatever their age. This kind of authority is the result of simply living. The authority of living always has greater influence than the authority of talking. A young person can possess all of the benefits of authority—influence, respect, and strength—just by living an ordinary life following Jesus wherever he leads.

Here's an easy way to know whether you have authority or not. If your friends ask for your advice, if they want to be with you when they are in crisis, if they refer their friends to you, if they defend you to others—then you know that they see you as someone with authority.

Rick is one of those very bright people other kids tolerate but don't like to hang out with. Rick knows all his "friends" at church put up with him because they need him now and then to fix their computers or bail them out at test time or to explain the latest calculus assignment. For some reason Rick never worries much about his nerd status. He has a lot of self-confidence and has no huge need to be cool. A lot of his confidence comes from his faith in Jesus.

Rick has always lived on the outside of life. His divorced parents have little time for him. He lives with his grandmother, who barely copes with her own arthritis and other old-age ailments. His brother and two sisters have long since gone their own ways—ways that are cluttered with drugs, alcohol, and repeated trouble. When Rick heard about Jesus and understood that Jesus not only died for him but also wanted him as a disciple, it was all Rick needed to hear. Not being wanted by anyone else only made Jesus' "wanting" of Rick more powerful in his life.

When Gina—the very popular and very sexy Gina—realized she was pregnant, it was Rick she asked for help and advice. When Mark—the very good-looking and very popular Mark—realized he was the father but didn't want to get married right away, he called Rick as well. Rick was surprised and, deep down inside himself, rather pleased. He realized that although his faith in Jesus Christ hadn't gotten rid of his nerdiness, it had given him authority.

The Obvious

When disciples use their authority, others are threatened by it.

[When was the last time you felt like you had authority?]

The Lesson

Wanna be a disciple? Then be prepared for resistance.

[How would you rephrase this Lesson?]

The Not-So-Obvious

Disciples of Christ are often misunderstood by other Christians.

[When was the last time you were misunderstood by another Christian?]

The Not-So-Obvious Lesson

A disciple is often in trouble, even in the church.

[What's something that could get you in trouble in your church—even if it's something you don't believe is a problem?]

for your write hand

• What did Rick's experience teach you about being a disciple?

• What would Jesus say to you right now about your authority?

exit poll

"If I walked into a group of my friends and they were having a discussion about sex, for example, and I said, 'The Bible makes it very clear that you can't have sex before marriage. You guys need to read your Bibles,' that would be the end of me. Even though I have the authority of God's word, I don't have any authority over my friends. Sorry—I just don't buy the idea that students can have authority."

BOLD

Matthew 10:34-39

Do not suppose that I have come to bring peace to the earth. I did not come to bring peace, but a sword. For I have come to turn "a man against his father, a daughter against her mother, a daughter-in-law against her mother-in-law—a man's enemies will be the members of his own household."

Anyone who loves his father or mother more than me is not worthy of me; anyone who loves his son or daughter more than me is not worthy of me; and anyone who does not take his cross and follow me is not worthy of me. Whoever finds his life will lose it, and whoever loses his life for my sake will find it.

Bold doesn't mean rude, obnoxious, loud, or disrespectful. Being bold is being firm, sure, confident, fearless, daring, strong, not easily intimidated, and resilient. It means you're willing to go where you've never been, willing to try what you've never tried, willing to trust what you've never trusted. Boldness is quiet, not noisy. Jesus' boldness in front of Pilate was his silence, but Pilate was blown away. Being bold is remaining firm when everyone around you yells at you to give in. Boldness is telling people what you believe even when your beliefs earn you ridicule. Boldness is a secret strength that others respect even when they act like they don't.

When you decide to follow God instead of following your friends, you are being bold. When you say no to your girlfriend or boyfriend because you are saying yes to God, you are being bold. Boldness isn't something you're born with. You either choose it or you don't.

Disciple Dilemma

LeAnne was excited. What a surprise this would be for her mom and dad! While finishing her senior year at high school she had written to Youth with a Mission and been accepted for discipleship training on the Mercy Ship, docked then in South Africa. She'd spend the summer raising the $6,000 she needed to fly to South Africa in September. Yes, she'd have to delay college for a few months, but YWAM and South Africa seemed like where God wanted LeAnne. Of course her parents would support her decision.

She couldn't have been more wrong. Her parents were hurt because she hadn't told them earlier about her plans. They were outraged that she was delaying going to college "after all they had done." Going to a nation with a recent history of political instability and racial conflict, they argued, was just plain dangerous. LeAnne's mom and dad made it very clear: South Africa was simply out of the question. Not an option. *School* was the only option. And frankly, they added, they had serious questions about the church LeAnne was attending and any youth program that would encourage such insanity.

Never in her 18 years had LeAnne felt so distant from her parents. They had always been supportive of everything she had done. They loved her youth group, loved her church. She was shocked, surprised, and shaken—and yet, she felt strangely calm inside. She heard herself saying, "I'm sorry you feel the way you do, Mom and Dad. I know you love me and I love you. I appreciate everything you have done for me. And I'm going to South Africa."

The Obvious
Being a disciple isn't easy.
[When was the last time you were bold about your faith?]

The Lesson
Following Jesus requires courage.
[Rate yourself on this Boldness Scale:]

Chicken_____Superhero

The Not-So-Obvious
Being a disciple is lonely.
[When was the last time you felt lonely because of your faith?]

The Not-So-Obvious Lesson
Being bold will make you enemies.
[Do you have any enemies because of your faith?]

for your write hand

• What did LeAnne's experience teach you about being a disciple?

• What would Jesus say to you right now about being bold?

exit poll

"Last time I checked, bold was not something I want to be. Obnoxious is another word for it. Who likes people who are in your face about anything—especially God? I believe it's much more effective to be silently bold by holding quietly to your beliefs."

CALLED

Matthew 4:18-20

As Jesus was walking beside the Sea of Galilee, he saw two brothers, Simon called Peter and his brother Andrew. They were casting a net into the lake, for they were fishermen. "Come, follow me," Jesus said, "and I will make you fishers of men." At once they left their nets and followed him.

Called is a strange word. You don't hear it much. You hear *career*, you hear *job*, you hear *interest*. People usually ask you about what you do, not what your calling is. But a calling is more than a job or career or something you do. A calling has to do with who you are. When God said to Jeremiah, "Before I formed you in the womb I knew you," he was talking about a calling (Jeremiah 1:5). A calling has to do with how we're made (read Psalm 139 for more on that). A calling is the place where your gifts, abilities, desires, meaning, and feelings of worth all meet. When you follow your calling, you feel at home, at peace—feel as though you're where you're meant to be.

A calling is always accompanied by passion. When you discover your calling, you'll be filled with joy, gratitude, and often tears. Your calling is the brand of God on your soul, the source of energy, renewal, and life. Disciples are more than people who believe in Jesus—they're people who *follow* him by listening to how they're made. A bunch of rugged fishermen with calloused hands that stunk of fish discovered that they were made for more than netting fish. They were made to fish for men and women.

disciple dilemma

Curt's not having a good time. With college just a month away, the question "What are you going to major in?" keeps coming up with more intensity.

"Look, Curt," his dad said firmly, "You can't keep floundering around trying to figure out what you're going to do with your life."

"I know, Dad. We've gone over the same ground all summer long. I just don't know what I want to do. All I know is that I want to do something for God, and I think that something is writing."

"Look, Curt, writing for God is fine. But you have to get your head out of the clouds and into the real world. I can make it easy for you to join my law firm. You can control the amount of hours you want to work in the practice, and the rest of the time you can write."

"Thanks, Dad. I mean, it all sounds sensible and reasonable, but sometimes God doesn't work sensibly and reasonably. Anyway, I don't need to decide right now. I don't have my head in the clouds. I'm just listening to my soul, to the way I'm made. You're good with words, Mom is an English teacher, and I'm only wanting to be what both of you made me to be—what *God* made me to be."

"Your mother and I did not make you a bum and neither did God, and that's what will happen to you if you keep being so fanatical."

"I am not a fanatic, Dad. I'm a Christian. I'm trying to follow Christ, just like you and Mom. At least that's why I thought you made sure I went to church. I can't believe you think I'm a fanatic."

"We went to church because we thought a little religion might provide a healthy environment for our family. We didn't think you'd go crazy."

"It's not crazy to follow the way you're made and it's not fanatical. I didn't 'get religion,' Dad. I found a way to honor the way you and Mom have raised me."

"If that's the way you honor your father and mother, then you'd better go back and read your Bible. You honor us by obeying us, and right now you're *dis*obeying us."

The Obvious

Disciples are called by God.

[Ever felt called by God to do something or be someone?]

The Lesson

Finding one's calling is the most important thing a disciple can do.

[How do you find your calling?]

The Not-So-Obvious

Following your calling can be very costly because it conflicts with others' expectations.

[In terms of your future, what expectations do your parents (or friends, or teachers) have of you?]

The Not-So-Obvious Lesson

Following Christ does not always make your circumstances better—it may make them worse.

[Do you honestly believe that following Christ will make your circumstances worse? Why or why not?]

for your write hand

• What did Curt's experience teach you about a calling?

• What would Jesus say to you right now about your calling?

exit poll

"I am called to follow Jesus and that is the most important goal of my life. I could care less about school. Jesus is coming back soon, and I'm not going to waste my time getting a so-called education. And forget about a job. God will provide. I am going to follow my calling and tell everyone I can about Jesus."

CLUELESS

Disciple Story

Matthew 26:6-13

While Jesus was in Bethany in the home of a man known as Simon the Leper, a woman came to him with an alabaster jar of very expensive perfume, which she poured on his head as he was reclining at the table.

When the disciples saw this, they were indignant. "Why this waste?" they asked. "This perfume could have been sold at a high price and the money given to the poor."

Aware of this, Jesus said to them, "Why are you bothering this woman? She has done a beautiful thing to me. The poor you will always have with you, but you will not always have me. When she poured this perfume on my body, she did it to prepare me for burial. I tell you the truth, wherever this gospel is preached throughout the world, what she has done will also be told, in memory of her."

Clueless means *oblivious*, which is a fancy word for unaware, unsuspecting, or caught by surprise. When you're clueless, you have no idea of what's going on. You don't understand what you're seeing or hearing. You know, like *duh*.

As far as God is concerned, most people assume that the longer you know him, the more you know *about* him. So maybe it's more accurate to say that the longer you know God, the less clueless you are, the less surprised you are by him. But it's also accurate to say the more you know about God, the more you realize how little you *really* know about him.

What does all this mean? It means that being a disciple is being clueless. As you spend more time with Jesus, you become less clueless about his ways and more aware of how mysterious he really is. Think about how exciting it is to be a disciple. Friendship with Jesus is a continuous growing process in which God becomes both more familiar and more mysterious at the same time.

Disciple Dilemma

Carver belonged to a downtown church with a mostly black congregation that lived in the south end of town. Southside was the most dangerous section of the city. Just about every week Southside was in the paper—a drive-by shooting, a murder, always some kind of violence.

Then the youth pastor of Creekwood Community Church invited Carver to come and speak to her suburban youth group. He was something of a celebrity among Creekwood's all-white congregation that Sunday as he explained how difficult it was to live where he did, when every night brought gunfire. The Creekwood kids were spellbound. When the floor was opened up for questions, they had no idea how stereotypical—even racist—their questions were.

"Must be difficult to grow up not knowing who your dad is," someone said, innocently.

Carver responded graciously, "Yeah, but I know who my mom is. She's an amazing person—tough, hardworking, and demanding. But I sure know how much she loves me and supports all that I do. I don't think many of you have a relationship with your mom like I do with mine."

"But isn't it scary living so close to gunfire every night?"

"Yes it is, but it's really helped me get closer to God. Not because I ask him to protect me, but more because I'm conscious of his presence with me. I don't think most white people feel that closeness more than once or twice in their lives."

"Yeah, but wouldn't you rather live in a peaceful area, away from all the violence and noise?"

"Oh, no, I'd *much* rather live in a place like mine," Carver shot back sarcastically. "Hell, of course I'd rather live where it's safe. But I can't. I won't leave my mom, and we can't afford to live somewhere else. It isn't like the movies, you know. Our neighborhood is family...we look out for each other. Look, I don't want to be mean or nothing, but it's tough living where I do and it's tough being black in a white society. But this Jesus thing's for real. He's been there for me, you know? He ain't got me out of the city. He ain't made my mom's life any easier, he ain't brought my dad back—but I know he's real. I wish I could explain what that means, but I can't."

The Obvious

The disciples were looking at the outside; Jesus was looking at the inside.

[When was the last time you felt clueless about your faith?]

The Lesson

Disciples look deeper than the exterior.

[Name some people you know whose interior is much different than their exterior.]

The Not-So-Obvious

Being clueless is the first step in growing.

[List some areas of your faith where you feel clueless.}

The Not-So-Obvious Lesson

Failures can teach you a lot.

[When was the last time you failed? What did you learn from it?]

for your write hand

• What did Carver's comments teach you about being a disciple?

• What would Jesus say to you right now about feeling clueless?

exit poll

"I'm the queen of clueless. I don't understand my faith like my other friends do. I have questions about everything. I even have questions about my questions. And I can tell everyone has lost patience with my questions. I can't help it—it's the way my mind works. I drove my parents crazy growing up. Actually, I still do. What's wrong with me? Why can't I be a good little Christian like everyone else and quit thinking of these questions?"

CONFUSED

Disciple story

Luke 22:14-23

When the hour came, Jesus and his apostles reclined at the table. And he said to them, "I have eagerly desired to eat this Passover with you before I suffer. For I tell you, I will not eat it again until it finds fulfillment in the kingdom of God."

After taking the cup, he gave thanks and said, "Take this and divide it among you. For I tell you I will not drink again of the fruit of the vine until the kingdom of God comes."

And he took bread, gave thanks and broke it, and gave it to them, saying, "This is my body given for you; do this in remembrance of me."

In the same way, after the supper he took the cup, saying, "This cup is the new covenant in my blood, which is poured out for you. But the hand of him who is going to betray me is with mine on the table. The Son of Man will go as it has been decreed, but woe to that man who betrays him." They began to question among themselves which of them it might be who would do this.

Confused means you're mixed-up, unclear. In other words, you don't get it. Confusion happens all the time. We don't understand what our parents mean, we don't understand the pastor's sermon, we don't understand a Bible verse, we don't understand what we're supposed to do next. Being confused is actually not so bad because it usually results in being unconfused. Often when you are confused you're on the brink of a new insight or new awareness.

Of course, when you are in the midst of confusion, you feel kind of stupid. You doubt yourself. You wonder whether you messed up or weren't listening to something important. Most of the time, though, confusion comes because we don't have all the pieces to the puzzle in front of us. So we just have to wait for more puzzle pieces. Meanwhile, don't apologize for being confused. Admit your confusion, learn from it, and start growing.

Disciple Dilemma

Trina thought she had prayer figured out. She had just finished a six-week study on the topic in her youth group. She learned that prayer isn't just asking for stuff from God; it's much more than that. It involves listening to God, opening up to him, talking with him. In other words, prayer is conversation, communion, connecting with God at a deep level. For years Trina had seen prayer as a way to get God to do what she wanted rather than as a way for God to get what he wanted from her.

Trina had prayed for years and years that her dad and mom wouldn't get a divorce. Unfortunately, last year they did divorce. Trina was now able to see that the divorce wasn't God's fault. She felt better about God than she had in years—until a few minutes ago, that is.

Jennifer had just called to share her excitement. "Trina, you will never believe what's happened. You know how my mom has cancer and everyone in the church has been praying for her? Well, she went to the doctor today to get the results of her

test, and the cancer is gone! The doctors can't understand what happened, but we know. God answered our prayers!"

Instead of being excited for Jennifer, Trina was angry. *God answered her prayer?* Trina asked herself. *Why didn't he answer my prayer? Why did I have to lose my family? What, I'm not a good enough Christian? I didn't pray enough? I didn't pray right? This prayer thing is a very cruel joke, and I don't get it.*

The Obvious
Confusion is a consequence of being a disciple.
[What are you confused about right now in your life?]

The Lesson
Confusion is an opportunity for growth.
[Can you remember a situation when you finally "got it" about God and saw your life change for the better?]

The Not-So-Obvious
We don't know ourselves very well.
[What is it about yourself that you don't understand—your anger? A weakness or inconsistency? A fear?]

The Not-So-Obvious Lesson
Being a disciple is learning to trust what Jesus knows more than trusting what you know.

Jesus knew who was with him and who was against him.

How would you describe yourself in relation to Jesus at this moment?

Kind of against him   In between   Sort of for him   Gung-ho for him

for your write hand

• What did Trina's experience with prayer teach you about being a disciple?

• What would Jesus say to you right now about being confused?

exit poll

"I don't get people who have all these questions about Christianity. Hey, Jesus is the answer, man. He doesn't give you more questions, he answers your questions. He's the Door, he's Life, he's the Living Water. People who have a bunch of questions just need to take them to Jesus. He'll answer them. That's why I'm a Christian. I don't need any more questions in my life. I need answers, and I found them in Jesus."

DARING

disciple story

Luke 5:17-26

One day as he was teaching, Pharisees and teachers of the law, who had come from every village of Galilee and from Judea and Jerusalem, were sitting there. And the power of the Lord was present for him to heal the sick. Some men came carrying a paralytic on a mat and tried to take him into the house to lay him before Jesus. When they could not find a way to do this because of the crowd, they went up on the roof and lowered him on his mat through the tiles into the middle of the crowd, right in front of Jesus.

When Jesus saw their faith, he said, "Friend, your sins are forgiven."

The Pharisees and the teachers of the law began thinking to themselves, "Who is this fellow who speaks blasphemy? Who can forgive sins but God alone?"

Jesus knew what they were thinking and asked, "Why are you thinking these things in your hearts? Which is easier: to say, 'Your sins are forgiven,' or to say, 'Get up and walk'? But that you may know that the Son of Man has authority on earth to forgive sins. . . ." He said to the paralyzed man, "I tell you, get up, take your mat and go home." Immediately he stood up in front of them, took what he had been lying on and went home praising God. Everyone was amazed and gave praise to God. They were filled with awe and said, "We have seen remarkable things today."

Daring is one characteristic of a disciple people don't talk about very much. It sounds so adventurous and—well, like Zorro. Daring people are kind of crazy, and daring disciples are kind of crazy for God. Being daring for God means being willing to go wherever Jesus wants to take us. Jesus wants us to touch people others say are untouchable? Okay. Jesus says we need to go into the temple and shake up the business leaders and religious dudes? Okay, I guess so. Jesus says it looks like things could get real dangerous? No problem. Daring is the quality in disciples that actually makes other people afraid of them. Daring disciples are truly different, and when you are different in this culture, you make others nervous.

disciple dilemma

My name is Jenine. Ariane, my best friend, and I will be graduating in two weeks. Ever since Ariane and I were in the seventh grade, we've had our lives planned. Neither one of us comes from a family with a lot of money. Both of us have to work during the summer to help with school costs. Luckily, both Ariane and I are good students—we received partial scholarships to Florida State University.

But just when I thought everything was looking great for this summer, Ariane flipped out. Out of nowhere she announced she's not getting a job. Instead, she's working with her church youth group and going with them on a mission trip to Haiti. It's crazy!

Now the plans we've made together for five years are ruined. Instead of going to FSU, where she has a scholarship, she's going to stay home and attend a local junior college part-time without a scholarship.

We've been good friends for a long time. I knew she went to church with her mom, but I didn't think she was serious about it. I mean, she's being so stupid! She's betraying our friendship, she's wasting a scholarship, and she's delaying her graduation from college (if she ever graduates) to help with a bunch of silly junior high kids at her church. Besides, going to Haiti is dangerous.

I've pleaded with Ariane to rethink what she's doing, but she won't listen. All of our friends have tried to talk to her. You know what she says? "Hey, you guys, I'm tired of our lives. All we do is go to movies, talk about boys, go out with boys, talk about more boys, try to look sexy, talk about sex, and go to school when we don't even know what we want to do. I'm bored with all that. I want to take some risks this summer. I want to help some kids. I want to help the poor. I'm not saying you guys are doing the wrong thing, but my faith is actually starting to sound exciting to me."

Can you believe Ariane? Her religion is exciting? I think she's lost it. I really do. She sounds like one of those Waco people to me. I'm glad I found this out about her now.

The Obvious
Faith isn't just a bunch of words, it's action.
[What actions do you use to express your faith?]

The Lesson
When faith is acted upon, people notice.
[On the following scale, indicate how much your faith is noticed by others.]

Not very often   Now and then   Quite a bit   A lot

The Not-So-Obvious
Daring things happen when disciples are focused.
[The friends of the paralyzed guy in the Bible story were so focused on getting the man to Jesus and getting him healed, they didn't think about what would happen when they tore apart someone's roof. Can you think of a time when you were so focused you didn't care what happened?]

The Not-So-Obvious Lesson
If you focus on Jesus first, he will help you deal with the consequences.
[Can you remember any instances when a possibly negative consequence of a decision kept you from doing the right thing?]

for your write hand

• What did Ariane's decision and her friends' reaction teach you about being a disciple?

• What would Jesus say to you right now about being daring?

exit poll

"I don't see why Christians have to be so in-your-face. People are so mean today, anyway, it seems like Christians ought to be nice. We should try to get along with people, not upset them. Christians shouldn't be running around making people mad, they should be making people glad."

DISCOURAGED

disciple story

Luke 24:13-27

Now that same day two of them were going to a village called Emmaus, about seven miles from Jerusalem. They were talking with each other about everything that had happened. As they talked and discussed these things with each other, Jesus himself came up and walked along with them; but they were kept from recognizing him.

He asked them, "What are you discussing together as you walk along?"

They stood still, their faces downcast. One of them, named Cleopas, asked him, "Are you the only one living in Jerusalem who doesn't know the things that have happened there in these days?"

"What things?" he asked.

"About Jesus of Nazareth," they replied. "He was a prophet, powerful in word and deed before God and all the people. The chief priests and our rulers handed him over to be sentenced to death, and they crucified him; but we had hoped that he was the one who was going to redeem Israel. And what is more, it is the third day since all this took place. In addition, some of our women amazed us. They went to the tomb early this morning but didn't find his body. They came and told us that they had seen a vision of angels, who said he was alive. Then some of our companions went to the tomb and found it just as the women had said, but him they did not see."

He said to them, "How foolish you are, and how slow of heart to believe all that the prophets have spoken! Did not the Christ have to suffer these things and then enter his glory?" And beginning with Moses and all the Prophets, he explained to them what was said in all the Scriptures concerning himself.

Discouraged isn't a bad thing, it's a normal thing. Discouragement is the shadow side of growing up. When your body is being attacked by hormones—like a teenager's body is—there are days when you just wake up feeling bad. The secret is to wait those kinds of days out, knowing things will get better. Then there are those days when feeling bad is justified. The two disciples in the story felt bad because life looked hopeless. Their faith in shambles, they had a million questions with no answers. So of course they felt bad. Though Jesus got a little frustrated with them, he also reminded the men of what they had forgotten. Then he had communion with them! Discouragement and discipleship go together. Because disciples believe intensely, they crash and burn intensely. Discouragement is part of being a disciple.

disciple dilemma

Every time I go to youth group I get the same response: "Hey, what's wrong with you?... Why so blue?...Lighten up!... Feeling all right?" Okay, I'll admit I'm moody. I feel sad a lot of the time. To be honest, the only time I feel absolutely exhilarated is when I'm dancing. I love ballet—I love any kind of dancing, really. Something happens to me when I dance. I know it sounds weird, but I feel close to God, I feel great about life, I feel like I'm on top of the world. Trouble is, when I go to our weekly Bible study on campus, everyone there thinks I'm not a very good Christian. They are always telling me to cheer up, to notify my face about how I should be feeling since I know Jesus. I'm a Christian, I'm trying to be a good one, but I'm not a very "up" person. Sometimes I wonder if Christianity is just for the I'm-always-happy people...or can someone like me be a follower of Christ?

The Obvious
Discouragement is part of being a disciple.
[When was the last time you were discouraged?]

The Lesson
Talking about your discouragement is a good way to get over it.
[Who do you have in your life that you can talk to about your discouragements?]

The Not-So-Obvious
Jesus helped the disciples through their discouragement. He read the Scriptures with them, and had communion with them.
[How can Jesus help you through your discouragement?]

The Not-So-Obvious Lesson
When you're discouraged, Jesus wants to be with you.
[How can Jesus be with you today?]

for your write hand

• What did the disciple dilemma teach you about being a disciple?

• What would Jesus say to you right now about discouragement?

exit poll

"Discouraged? I'm always discouraged. Seems like I can never get this Christian thing right. I'm always blowing it. I'm always feeling bad about my life. Trust me—some of us are disciple material, some of us aren't."

DOUBTING

Disciple Story

John 20:24-29

Now Thomas (called Didymus), one of the Twelve, was not with the disciples when Jesus came. When the other disciples told him that they had seen the Lord, he declared, "Unless I see the nail marks in his hands and put my finger where the nails were, and put my hand into his side, I will not believe it."

A week later his disciples were in the house again, and Thomas was with them. Though the doors were locked, Jesus came and stood among them and said, "Peace be with you!" Then he said to Thomas, "Put your finger here; see my hands. Reach out your hand and put it into my side. Stop doubting and believe."

Thomas said to him, "My Lord and my God!"

Then Jesus told him, "Because you have seen me, you have believed; blessed are those who have not seen and yet have believed."

Doubting means having questions that keep you from believing. To doubt is often to be very brave, because believers usually don't like doubters. Not *all* doubters are brave, though. Lazy doubters merely use their questions to avoid the responsibility of belief. Cynical doubters question everything just because they like to shake everyone else's beliefs. We doubt when we don't know, we doubt when we are afraid to know, and we doubt when we don't want to know. Most of the time disciples doubt because they are confused or lost.

Thomas was willing to die as a disciple of Christ (John 11:16). Yet because he didn't want a secondhand faith, he doubted whether the disciples had seen Jesus. He wanted to touch the resurrected Jesus himself as proof. And Jesus didn't banish Thomas for doubting, but instead honored his doubts by actually showing up and giving Thomas the proof he demanded. To Thomas and to you, Jesus says, "I wish you didn't doubt, but I love you because your faith is so important that you are brave enough to ask the questions of your soul."

Disciple Dilemma

Before she gave her life to God about a year ago, Juanita's grades were barely above C's, her relationship with her parents was terrible, she was hanging around drug dealers and users—Juanita was close to disaster.

But everything is different now. Juanita's grades are better, she has a new group of friends (mostly from youth group), and she stays home to help her parents around the house because both of them work. Yet Juanita's parents refuse to talk about God with her—not to mention never going to church with her.

"We're not talking to you about God, Juanita," they said more than once. "Sorry, but that's the end of it."

She had been praying for her parents for a year now, but nothing changed with her parents. Juanita became discouraged and even began doubting that Christianity was for real after all.

She woke up early on her birthday because her parents wanted to celebrate before she went to church. Breakfast was fun—18 sausage candles on a stack of her favorite pancakes. Her parents' present to her was no package, but a small envelope. Juanita opened it, unfolded a single sheet, and recognized her father's handwriting.

Dear Juanita,

You remember Grandma Breck talking about the death of my older brother—your uncle you never knew. What you've never been told is that he was about 16. He committed suicide. When my parents went to the church to ask for a funeral, they were told that they didn't give enough money. Besides, the church leaders said, suicide was a sin.

My parents never went back to church. Neither did I. I hated God and I hated religion. About a year ago, as you know, your mother and I were at the end of our rope over you—and then you suddenly changed. But when you told us Jesus was the reason, I couldn't handle it. All the memories and bitterness came back. But during the past few months you've been so different that I realized whatever had happened had to be real. I knew you wanted us to say something, but my anger just wouldn't let me. Counseling helped some. (Yes, that's where I've been Thursday nights for the last two months!) So your mother and I have thought and talked a lot about it, and decided to give you the birthday present you want: we'll go to church with you starting this morning. We won't become instant saints, but if we can be anything like you we'll be happy.

The Obuious
It's okay to doubt.
[Do you have many doubts? List some of them.]

The Lesson
Don't be afraid to bring your doubts to Jesus.
[Have you brought your doubts to Jesus? Did it do any good?]

The Not-So-Obuious
Jesus is not afraid of our questions.
[Do you feel comfortable going to Jesus with your questions? Why or why not?]

The Not-So-Obuious Lesson
Don't let anyone convince you that your questions show a lack of faith. The opposite is true. Your questions are symptoms of a growing and active faith.
[Do you think a disciple of Christ should have doubts?]

for your write hand

• What did Juanita's experience with her parents teach you about being a disciple?

• What would Jesus say to you right now about doubting?

exit poll

"Faith is believing even when you have questions. A good Christian should believe God no matter what. Questions and doubts are tools of the devil. Questions are for weaklings. Believing Christians have no doubts about God. It's that simple."

EMOTIONAL

Disciple Story

Matthew 17:1-9

After six days Jesus took with him Peter, James and John the brother of James, and led them up a high mountain by themselves. There he was transfigured before them. His face shone like the sun, and his clothes became as white as the light. Just then there appeared before them Moses and Elijah, talking with Jesus.

Peter said to Jesus, "Lord, it is good for us to be here. If you wish, I will put up three shelters—one for you, one for Moses and one for Elijah."

While he was still speaking, a bright cloud enveloped them, and a voice from the cloud said, "This is my Son, whom I love; with him I am well pleased. Listen to him!"

When the disciples heard this, they fell facedown to the ground, terrified. But Jesus came and touched them. "Get up," he said. "Don't be afraid." When they looked up, they saw no one except Jesus.

As they were coming down the mountain, Jesus instructed them, "Don't tell anyone what you have seen, until the Son of Man has been raised from the dead."

Emotional means passionate, excitable, intense. It can also mean fickle, unstable, temperamental, and unpredictable. When people are so in touch with their emotions that they listen to their feelings instead of their reason, they can sometimes end up in trouble. But reason can get us into trouble, too. Reason and logic can keep us from experiencing the highs and lows of life that should be experienced by everyone, especially a follower of Jesus.

On the other hand, emotions can be shallow and manipulative. Emotional people often *use* their emotions instead of experiencing and listening to those emotions. A girl may cry when her boyfriend breaks up with her because she is genuinely sad or she may cry because she hopes her tears will cause her boyfriend to decide to stay in the relationship. An angry guy may find a way to resolve his anger or he may decide to act on it. He may use his anger to right a wrong or he may give into the anger and create another wrong. Strong emotions can give us the strength to persevere or become the basis of giving up. Emotional people are usually up and down a lot—but they also hug a lot, too.

Disciple Dilemma

"God is so awesome!" Terry was in the middle of his testimony. "I just want to tell all of you that God is just so awesome! I've only been a Christian for about a year now, but I just can't believe how awesome God is! Every day I wake up and say, "God, you are really awesome! Hey, don't you all agree? I look around at the guys I used to run around with. I look at most of the kids on our campus, and I think to myself, *God, you are really awesome!* If all my friends could know how awesome God is, what a difference it would make. So I just want you to know how totally awesome God is!"

When Terry sat down Diane, the youth group skeptic, stood up. "Terry, I'm excited that you think God is great. But what exactly did you just say? I have no idea what you were talking about. You said God was awesome, but never once did you say why! You just kept repeating that God is awesome. To be honest, it sounded more like a cheer than a testimony. Forgive me, Terry, I don't mean to hurt your feelings or anything. You know I think you're a neat guy, but don't you think we have to have some reasons for our faith other than just repeating one word over and over again?"

The youth group didn't know how to respond. Some were angry at Diane. Some had no idea what she was talking about. Some agreed with her, even though they didn't want to hurt Terry's feelings.

The Obvious
Our emotions cannot always be trusted.

[When was the last time you got emotional?]

The Lesson
Disciples listen to their emotions and listen to reason.

[Any ideas on how you can listen to reason while your emotions are screaming?]

The Not-So-Obvious
Jesus' sense of call helped him know what to do and when to do it.

[Let's say you're passionately involved with someone of the opposite sex and your emotions are saying, "Go for it!" How can your "call" to follow Jesus help you at that moment?]

The Not-So-Obvious Lesson
Disciples must try to remember Jesus' call on their lives during messy situations.

[When was the last time you were in a messy situation?]

for your write hand

• What did Terry's testimony and Diane's criticism teach you about being a disciple?

• What would Jesus say to you right now about your emotions?

exit poll

"Just what is wrong with emotions? I trust them a lot more than my mind. There are too many people trying to think about their faith and talk about what it means. I want a faith that is sensual, a faith that I can experience. I want to feel God, not intellectualize about him."

FRIENDLY

disciple story

John 15:11-17

"I have told you this so that my joy may be in you and that your joy may be complete. My command is this: Love each other as I have loved you. Greater love has no one than this, that he lay down his life for his friends. You are my friends if you do what I command. I no longer call you servants, because a servant does not know his master's business. Instead, I have called you friends, for everything that I learned from my Father I have made known to you. You did not choose me, but I chose you and appointed you to go and bear fruit—fruit that will last. Then the Father will give you whatever you ask in my name. This is my command: Love each other."

Friendly, as much as *follower* and *learner*, describes a disciple. A disciple is a friend, a confidant, someone who is trusted, a companion, a person who comes alongside. Friends share their lives with each other, talk about everything, reveal their deepest secrets. Friends know how to listen, how to be with each other without saying a word. Friends do not just care for a common cause, they care for each other.

Disciples follow Jesus' teachings; friends follow Jesus' heart. Disciples will die for the truth; friends will die for each other. Disciples spend a lot of time together, getting to know each other, building their relationship and not just their beliefs. Disciples who are friends know the meaning of relationship and community. They understand that Christianity is not an isolated adventure; it involves making friends with the friends of Jesus.

disciple dilemma

The youth pastor at New Life Community Church was really cool. He was funny, good-looking, a great communicator, and a lover of Jesus. Everyone liked Greg and his wife, Lindy. He spent hours just hanging out with us kids. He was really fun to be around, teasing and joking and generally being the center of attention, which no one minded because he knew how to show us a good time. And when it came to talking about Jesus, you could tell Greg really cared about us. He had such a passion for Jesus that you couldn't help but want the same thing.

I don't know how many times Greg had the youth group in tears because of our lack of commitment. I really think all of us wanted to be just like Greg. He was so happy, so on fire, so cool. He used to tell us that he and his wife didn't need adult friends because the youth group kids were his friends.

Then the news broke about his affair. At first none of us believed it. It was crazy. Greg disappeared for a couple weeks, but we were sure that he'd come back and the whole affair thing would be disproved. But he didn't. It turned out that Greg not only had an affair with Deena— a girl in our youth group, barely 18—but he had left town with her, leaving Lindy alone and devastated.

First we were shocked, then we got angry. We sat around for hours trying to figure out what went wrong. Sure, we don't know the whole story, but we knew one thing: Greg was really a stranger to us, a loner. He had no friends, really. He said *we* were his friends, but he never talked to us about his life and he never let us talk to him about ours. He preached to us, but he was far from a friend. We remembered that he said he didn't need adult friends. Now we know why. Friends know you, and if he'd had a friend his affair would have been found out in the beginning.

I know there's got to be more to the story than this. Our youth group is in shambles. We've tried to be there for Lindy, but it's kind of awkward. We heard she's going to another church. None of us will ever be the same after this betrayal, but I'll tell you one thing about our youth group: we sure have become good friends.

The Obvious
A disciple is a friend of Jesus and a friend of other disciples.
[Do you have a lot of friends? Why or why not?]

The Lesson
Making friends is an important part of being a disciple.
[Before now, did you ever think friendship was part of being a disciple? Why or why not?]

The Not-So-Obvious
Friendships don't just happen; they're a choice.
[When you hear Jesus' statement, "You did not choose me, but I chose you," how does it make you feel?]

The Not-So-Obvious Lesson
Choosing and maintaining friendships is hard work. Disciples are committed to the hard work of friendship.
[What does this statement mean to you: "Friendships are hard work"?]

for your write hand

• What did the youth group's dilemma teach you about being a disciple?

• What would Jesus say to you right now about being a friend?

exit poll

"Jesus hung around the disciples, yes, but most of the time he was alone. He often left his 'friends' to be alone. You may have friends, but in the end you're alone. Look at Jesus. Where were all his disciples when he died? He died alone. So friends are fine, but I'm trusting no one but me and God. What's wrong with that?"

X

12

GENEROUS

Disciple story

John 13:4-5, 12-17

Jesus got up from the meal, took off his outer clothing, and wrapped a towel around his waist. After that, he poured water into a basin and began to wash his disciples' feet, drying them with the towel that was wrapped around him.

When he had finished washing their feet, he put on his clothes and returned to his place. "Do you understand what I have done for you?" he asked them. "You call me 'Teacher' and 'Lord,' and rightly so, for that is what I am. Now that I, your Lord and Teacher, have washed your feet, you also should wash one another's feet. I have set you an example that you should do as I have done for you. I tell you the truth, no servant is greater than his master, nor is a messenger greater than the one who sent him. Now that you know these things, you will be blessed if you do them."

Generous describes disciples in this way: they're more than doers. They're givers. And it's more than mere words and knowledge that disciples give to others. Disciples give *themselves* to others. Disciples serve others by listening, supporting, encouraging, affirming, confronting, helping, loving, empathizing, and being there. Disciples are generous with their time and energy, imitating the One who knew how to serve. As servants, disciples learn how to be sensitive, to know when they are needed and when they are not needed. True servants can read people well. They can feel pain in others and know when to step in and help. True servanthood is very difficult, yet very important because it is the one unmistakable way people recognize Jesus in us (Matthew 25:34-46).

Disciple Dilemma

Every month Daryl's youth group went to Beverly Manor to conduct a church service for the elderly. Daryl didn't like to go, but he felt obligated. *That's what Jesus would do,* Daryl thought, *even though Jesus didn't have old-folks homes in his day. Lucky him!*

After five services at the Manor, he still really hadn't done anything—just stood in the back of the room and held Oliver's hand. Oliver was in his eighties or nineties, seldom spoke, and usually slept through the church service. Daryl liked the old guy, though. Sometimes Daryl would nudge him awake and talk to to him, though Oliver never seemed to listen. Still, whenever Daryl was about to leave, Oliver squeezed Daryl's hand, and in response Daryl would always lean down and whisper in Oliver's ear, "Sorry, Oliver, but I gotta go. But I love you,

and I'll be back next month. I promise." Daryl had never told anyone else this.

Then came the day Daryl arrived at the Manor, looked for Oliver as usual, but couldn't see him. He went to the head nurse. "I don't see Oliver here today," he said. "Is he okay?"

Daryl followed the nurse to a room in the clinic. And there Oliver lay, looking more frail than ever, his eyes closed, his breathing irregular. Daryl walked over and took his hand. He had never seen anyone dying before. For an hour Daryl sat with Oliver. Then as he moved in his chair to stand, he felt the familiar squeeze of Oliver's hand. For the last time, Daryl leaned over to Oliver's ear and whispered, "Sorry, but I gotta go. I love you."

It was probably because his eyes were wet that he almost collided with a twenty-something female

headed into Oliver's room. She looked at Daryl kind of funny.

"Uh, sorry," he said. "I'm Daryl. I'm, uh, kind of a friend of Oliver's." He paused. "He's dying, you know.

"Yes, I know," the girl said. "I'm his granddaughter. I was hoping to meet you...see, I came to see Grandpa a couple weeks ago when the doctors said he was dying. He sort of woke up and said to me, 'Say goodbye to Jesus for me.' I told him that he was going to be with Jesus soon. And he said, 'I know, but he comes to see me every month and he might not know I've gone.' Later I asked the nurse if she had any idea what he meant and she told me that you came once a month with a youth group, and held his hand.

"I imagine Jesus is very glad to have been mistaken for you."

The Obvious
Disciples are generous servants.
[What do you think it means for you to be a generous servant?]

The Lesson
Serving others is a choice.
[When was the last time you chose to serve someone?]

The Not-So-Obvious
Serving others is embarrassing and hard.
[What is "embarrassing and hard" about service?]

The Not-So-Obvious Lesson
We will always meet Jesus when we generously serve others.
[What does the statement above mean to you?]

for your write hand

• What did Daryl's experience with Oliver teach you about being a disciple?

• What would Jesus say to you right now about being a servant?

exit poll

"You know why I like to serve people? Because it makes me feel good. When I serve others less fortunate than me I'm always thankful I'm not like them. It always makes me appreciate all the cool stuff I have. I think it's great to serve others because it makes me glad I'm not them."

HATED

Disciple story

John 15:18-25

"If the world hates you, keep in mind that it hated me first. If you belonged to the world, it would love you as its own. As it is, you do not belong to the world, but I have chosen you out of the world. That is why the world hates you. Remember the words I spoke to you: 'No servant is greater than his master.' If they persecuted me, they will persecute you also. If they obeyed my teaching, they will obey yours also. They will treat you this way because of my name, for they do not know the One who sent me. If I had not come and spoken to them, they would not be guilty of sin. Now, however, they have no excuse for their sin. He who hates me hates my Father as well. If I had not done among them what no one else did, they would not be guilty of sin. But now they have seen these miracles, and yet they have hated both me and my Father. But this is to fulfill what is written in their Law: 'They hated me without reason.'"

Hated can come in the form of criticism, ridicule, or sarcasm. It can take the shape of rejection, hostility, or avoidance. Those who hate you find ways to hurt you, ways to make you feel stupid, ways to make it look as though you're at fault. Hateful people know how to convince everyone around them that they are your friend while they slowly twist a knife in your back.

Hatred can take the form of "godly" behavior as well. People can hide behind their religion and use it as a weapon to demolish you and your reputation. Hatred is pure evil. It can destroy people very quickly. What is frightening about hatred is that those who hate feel no remorse. They feel good. They feel righteous and legitimate. They feel justified in their hatred. Good people are often most hurt because they're not prepared for how vicious and ugly hatred can be. Hatred can be triggered quickly when people feel threatened or in danger of losing power. Jesus made it very clear that people are capable of hating nice, godly disciples just as they were capable of hating the sinless, loving Son of God.

Disciple Dilemma

"Get the hell out of here!" Jessie's dad was an alcoholic and right now he was recovering from one of his binges. The binge would usually start with Jessie's father verbally abusing anyone in sight. Eventually, as he drank more, he would leave for three or four days (which was a relief for everyone). Then he would return home remorseful, guilt-ridden, crying, vowing never to drink again. It wasn't unusual for Jessie's dad to use such language when he was recovering from a binge.

"Dad, I'm not getting the hell out of here!" Jessie said. "I am trying to tell you that Jesus is the only one who can help you. I know. I started drinking my junior year and realized it was a black hole. A friend of mine told me about Jesus and I stopped. You can stop, too, and you *need* to stop before you lose all of us."

"Look, Billy Graham," his dad replied. "I don't need you telling me what to do. I don't need some smart-ass teenager acting like he knows more than I do about life. You seem to forget that my dad was a preacher! He loved Jesus, all right, but he also loved his bottle. The only difference between him and me is that he was able to hide it from all those "good church people." Jesus didn't help my dad, he ain't going to help me, and he ain't helping you. Just because you haven't had a drink for a few days doesn't mean nothing. And you know what else, son? Religion is a bunch of crap, and no son of mine is going to become some Bible-toting fanatic. You hear me?"

"Dad, I just want you to get some help," Jessie said.

"No you don't," his dad corrected. "You just want me to get out of here so you can run things and make everyone in the family a Jesus fanatic. Let me make it as clear as I can for you, son. I hate God and I hate religion. All it did for me was pay for my father's booze. You keep going down this Jesus trail and I'll tell you right now, son, I'll end up hating you, too. If you cared about me you wouldn't have anything to do with Jesus. Period."

The Obvious

A disciple of Christ can expect to be hated by some people.

[Hate is a strong word. Have you known anyone to ever hate you? Have you ever hated someone? What did it feel like?]

The Lesson

Don't sacrifice your faith in order to be liked by everyone.

[Do you think if you really lived your faith all the time, some of your friendships might be in jeopardy? Why or why not?]

The Not-So-Obvious

Evangelism does more than point to the light, it exposes the darkness.

[Have you ever been nervous around "darkness"? Did you feel like your faith was obvious to those who were in the darkness? If so, did your faith make others uncomfortable?]

The Not-So-Obvious Lesson

Disciples are not surprised by their enemies—they are prepared for them.

[How should Christians prepare for their enemies?]

for your write hand

• What did Jessie's conversation with his father teach you about being a disciple?

• What would Jesus say to you right now about being hated?

exit poll

"Jesus is so cool that if people really know who he is and how much he loves them, they will follow him. Our faith doesn't have to make enemies. In fact, our faith ought to make tons of friends. Even if others don't accept Jesus, they have to like Christians. Why would they hate someone they can trust, someone who just wants to do good? I love Jesus with all my heart and I don't have any enemies. In fact, since I became a Christian, I have more friends than ever."

HUMAN

Matthew 20:20-24

Then the mother of Zebedee's sons came to Jesus with her sons and, kneeling down, asked a favor of him.

"What is it you want?" he asked.

She said, "Grant that one of these two sons of mine may sit at your right and the other at your left in your kingdom."

"You don't know what you are asking," Jesus said to them. "Can you drink the cup I am going to drink?"

"We can," they answered.

Jesus said to them, "You will indeed drink from my cup, but to sit at my right or left is not for me to grant. These places belong to those for whom they have been prepared by my Father."

When the ten heard about this, they were indignant with the two brothers.

Human means that when you decide to follow Christ, you may leave your past behind—but you bring with you your friends, your family, your humanity—complete with idiosyncrasies and flaws. When you bring yourself to Jesus, that self is attached to a whole lot of stuff—your physical looks, for example, and your emotional makeup and personality and family and financial situation, to name just a few. This stuff complicates your decision to follow Jesus. For example, say you have a quick temper. So when you decide to follow Jesus, the "you" that follows Jesus also has a quick temper (kind of like Peter). Or you may have an alcoholic parent. Now that you're a Christian, you *still* have an alcoholic parent—or an overprotective mother or a ridiculously strict stepfather or a redneck brother. If your family was in any way weird before you decided to follow Christ, it's *still* weird after Jesus comes into your life. James and John had an aggressive mother who wanted her boys to have the best, who felt she had to look out for her "little boys." James and John simply had to deal with this uncomfortable reality. Jesus had to deal with it, too.

Disciple Dilemma

Jon is one of those students who dreads school. Every day he's forced to attend a place where—in his experience—each class, each homework assignment, almost all interaction is negative. Jon has been tested, retested, and tested again. Experts examined him for dyslexia, then vision problems, then hearing problems. Turns out Jon is just a slow learner. Whatever that means. Of course, having someone *tell* you that you learn slowly doesn't help much. In fact, it makes things worse. Now everyone knows Jon is a slow learner. At school he's treated with pity and sympathy instead of like a normal person—which he is, other than the fact that it takes him longer to learn than others.

One week a friend invited Jon to church the next Sunday. He actually liked the kids in the youth group. They accepted him, and he wasn't put into situations where his "slow learner" stuff was obvious. Not long afterwards Jon decided to become a Christian. The youth pastor had been saying for months that Jesus would not only save Jon's soul, but would be the answer to his problems. Jon still remembers the night he said yes to Jesus. The next day he felt like he was walking on air. He breezed through school and began to believe that because of his new faith, his problems would disappear—especially his slow learning. For three

months Jon grew in his faith like crazy. He went to weekly Bible studies, shared his faith with others, and even got along with his parents better. Jon just *knew* that with Jesus his school work would turn around.

About that time Jon received an urgent referral from his school. The counseling department recommended that Jon be held back a year and reassigned to a special learning class.

Thanks a lot, Jesus, Jon thought bitterly. *You really know how to solve my problems.*

The Obvious

Your humanness complicates your walk with Christ.

[When was the last time your humanity got in the way of your faith?]

The Lesson

Jesus expects disciples to be human.

[What does being human mean?]

The Not-So-Obvious

Everyone was ticked off at the disciples—except Jesus.

[When was the last time you felt like Jesus was ticked off at you?]

The Not-So-Obvious Lesson

Jesus expects more failure from you than you do.

[Where would you put yourself on the failure scale below?]

Fail all the time _____ Rarely fail

for your write hand

• What did Jon's experience teach you about humanity?

• What would Jesus say to you right now about your humanness?

exit poll

"Humanness is the opposite of godliness. When you justify your humanity, you're going too far. Sure we're human, but we don't have to give in to it—and we certainly don't have to condone our humanity. Yes, disciples are human—but they're supposed to be godly. End of story."

HUNGRY

wwjd

disciple story

John 1:35-39

The next day John was there again with two of his disciples. When he saw Jesus passing by, he said, "Look, the Lamb of God!"

When the two disciples heard him say this, they followed Jesus. Turning around, Jesus saw them following and asked, "What do you want?"

They said, "Rabbi" (which means Teacher), "where are you staying?"

"Come," he replied, "and you will see."

So they went and saw where he was staying, and spent that day with him. It was about the tenth hour.

Hungry disciples crave truth, yearn for it. Those who sincerely want to know more, to grow more are driven by their passion for truth. A disciple is much more than a student or apprentice. A disciple isn't satisfied with knowing more—a disciple wants to know it *all*, to experience it *all*. Disciples' longing for truth makes them willing learners, eager followers with an insatiable hunger for knowledge. That hunger is aggressive, pursuing, and relentless. Hungry disciples are energized by their appetite and eagerly enlist others to search for truth with them. When you lose your appetite for truth, when you stop being hungry for God, then you become comfortable and lazy. Hunger is a quality that is central to what a disciple is.

disciple dilemma

Trina is confused. She used to attend Bible study every week and youth group every Sunday night. She loved learning about God and was thinking seriously about attending a Bible college when she graduates next year. But during the summer she found a good job waitressing at a trendy restaurant. Because Trina looks much older than her 18 years and the customers like her, the owners of the restaurant like her. The money she makes is so good, in fact, that she convinced her dad to let her buy a car. When school began, though,

Trina needed to work weekends to keep up with her car payments. The rest of the time she spent trying to maintain her 4.0 GPA. It wasn't easy. Something had to go.

One night on her way to work, she realized church and youth group didn't sound all that good anymore. So she stopped going. It certainly promised to make Trina's schedule easier. Now, three months later, she figured that all that "get on fire for God" stuff had begun to turn her off, anyway. And she began to dread the Bible like she dreaded the dentist.

What's crazy is that Trina was so into God just three months ago. She was reading her Bible, praying for her friends, and thinking about the Lord all the time. She didn't think her enthusiasm for God would ever change. But it had.

Oh well, Trina thought. *As soon as my senior year is over I'll get back into my faith. Right now I need to pay my bills and keep my grades up. That's the most important issue for me.*

The Obvious
The disciples' hunger for Jesus was matched by Jesus' desire for them.
[What part of your faith are you "hungry" to know about?]

The Lesson
Spending time with Jesus is the way disciples grow.
[When's the last time you spent time with Jesus? What did you do?]

The Not-So-Obvious
John's disciples quit following John and started following Jesus.
[John gave up his own followers, his own loyal disciples. What are you willing to give up to follow Jesus—relationships with parents? With friends? Money? Future security?]

The Not-So-Obvious Lesson
Spending more time with Jesus always means you spend less time doing something else.
[What could you spend less time doing in order to spend more time with Jesus?]

for your write hand

• What did Trina's change of heart teach you about hunger for spiritual things?

• What would Jesus say to you right now about your hunger for God?

exit poll

"Hunger is such a weird word. Like any friend I know says, 'I'm hungry for God.' Let's get on the same planet here, okay? Nobody I know is 'hungry' for God, and I'm not either. Sure, I'd like to be a nice person and help people, but I'm a busy girl. I'm sure God understands."

IMMATURE

disciple story

Matthew 14:22-33

Immediately Jesus made the disciples get into the boat and go on ahead of him to the other side, while he dismissed the crowd. After he had dismissed them, he went up into the hills by himself to pray. When evening came, he was there alone, but the boat was already a considerable distance from land, buffeted by the waves because the wind was against it.

During the fourth watch of the night Jesus went out to them, walking on the lake. When the disciples saw him walking on the lake, they were terrified. "It's a ghost," they said, and cried out in fear.

But Jesus immediately said to them: "Take courage! It is I. Don't be afraid."

"Lord, if it's you," Peter replied, "tell me to come to you on the water."

"Come," he said.

Then Peter got down out of the boat and walked on the water to Jesus. But when he saw the wind, he was afraid and, beginning to sink, cried out, "Lord, save me!"

Immediately Jesus reached out his hand and caught him. "You of little faith," he said, "why did you doubt?"

And when they climbed into the boat, the wind died down. Then those who were in the boat worshiped him, saying, "Truly you are the Son of God."

Immature can mean foolish, naive, silly, childish. When people want to criticize a young person, they often use a word like *immature* to communicate dissatisfaction with certain kinds of behavior. Immaturity usually means people are not behaving appropriately, not "acting their age," not acting grown up. Often you'll hear an adult yell in exasperation, "Grow up!" by which the adult usually means, "Quit acting like a kid!" But immaturity is not always bad. It suggests being young, enthusiastic, energetic, undeveloped, inexperienced, or uninformed. Sometimes our immaturity is what causes us to try new ways of living, new ways of thinking, and new ways of believing. Immaturity often drives us to try new things, to risk more, to live fearlessly, even dangerously. Immaturity produces adventures and accidents, wild surprises and humiliating failure. All of Jesus' disciples were immature. You have to be immature before you can be mature. It was during their immature years that the disciples did the most, learned the most, and put their lives in the most danger.

disciple dilemma

Marlena was very frustrated. Here she was, 16 years old, standing in front of the leaders of her church, and she could tell they were angry with her. All she did was stand up in the annual meeting to ask why the church was moving out of the inner city to the suburbs. The meeting was being held to approve the new plan to buy a piece of property in a beautiful area just outside of town. Someone had donated a few million dollars for the church to move out of the crime-infested, rapidly deteriorating old part of town. Marlena's family lived just a few

blocks from where the new church would be built, but she still couldn't understand the decision. "Listen to me, please, everyone. I know I'm young. I know what I give to the church is a drop in the bucket. I know I'm just a kid, but we can't do this. We can't abandon this part of the city. Think of what we could do with the millions of dollars we're talking about if we invested it in the people who live all around us!"

The minister stood to his feet. "Thanks, Marlena, we really do appreciate your input, but when you get older you'll understand. Dr.

Kerry Dawson is a long-time member of this church and his very gracious offer of three million dollars was made on the condition that we move. It would be a sin to turn down that amount of money."

"But, Pastor," Marlena said tearfully, "why don't we just ask him to give the money here instead?"

The entire congregation laughed. The vote was nearly unanimous to take the money and move. Marlena cast the only "no" vote.

The Obvious
Peter's immaturity caused him to walk on water and sink at the same time.
[Where are you on the immaturity scale below?]

Very Immature   More Mature Than Average

The Lesson
Immature disciples make big mistakes and have big adventures.
[What was the last "adventure" you had with God?]

The Not-So-Obvious
Peter not only had to walk on water, he had to do it under windy conditions.
[Looking at your situation right now, what are the windy conditions in your life? Divorce? Stepparents? Girlfriend/Boyfriend? Money?]

The Not-So-Obvious Lesson
When you follow Jesus, don't expect Jesus to eliminate all of your problems.
[What problems in your life would you like eliminated?]

for your write hand

• What did Marla's confrontation at church teach you about being a disciple?

• What would Jesus say to you right now about your immaturity?

exit poll
"I am immature and proud of it. I am 15 and I don't have to be mature, whatever that means. If I have to be mature to be a Christian, then take my name off the list because it ain't going to happen. We have a bunch of adults at our church who are always getting bent out of shape because we act immature in church. 'Act your age,' they say. I want to yell back, 'I am, you idiot!'"

INCAPABLE

disciple story

Matthew 17:1-2, 14-21

After six days Jesus took with him Peter, James and John the brother of James, and led them up a high mountain by themselves. There he was transfigured before them. His face shone like the sun, and his clothes became as white as the light. . . .

When they came to the crowd, a man approached Jesus and knelt before him. "Lord, have mercy on my son," he said. "He is an epileptic and is suffering greatly. I brought him to your disciples, but they could not heal him."

"O unbelieving and perverse generation," Jesus replied, "how long shall I stay with you? How long shall I put up with you? Bring the boy here to me." Jesus rebuked the demon, and it came out of the boy, and he was healed from that moment.

Then the disciples came to Jesus in private and asked, "Why couldn't we drive it out?"

He replied, "Because you have so little faith. I tell you the truth, if you have faith as small as a mustard seed, you can say to this mountain, 'Move from here to there' and it will move. Nothing will be impossible for you."

Incapable means you're unable to do something you want to do. It means you're in over your head, trapped by your circumstances, bewildered, confused, or just plain lost. Sometimes people are incapable because they haven't been trained properly, they don't possess the necessary skills, or they don't have enough experience.

In the story above the disciples had just come down from a mountain where they had an unbelievable experience. They'd seen Jesus become transparent right in front of them! Not only that, they'd seen Moses and Elijah appear right in front of their eyes! What an experience! They were on top of the world. Then they came down the mountain and couldn't heal a little boy. They were frustrated, of course, but Jesus pointed out that healing little boys takes a lot of faith and a lot of time. Not everyone can heal little boys. The power comes from God, but the faith comes from us.

Disciples can't do everything. Being a disciple doesn't guarantee success. Disciples have to learn and work and spend a lot of time alone with Jesus. Being incapable doesn't mean we can't be a disciple, it just means we have a lot to learn.

disciple dilemma

During the last two years Sue had watched her friend Darci become very active in a local church, attend Bible studies every week, and really try to live her faith. Sue, however, wasn't a Christian and didn't think the Jesus thing was for her. She just didn't feel like God would accept her because of—well, because of *things* that had happened in her life,

Darci was especially bubbly today. Just back from a youth group retreat, she went on and on about her relationship with God. "Sue, we've been friends now for two years," said Darci. "You've seen what Jesus has done in my life. Why don't you see what Jesus

can do in yours?"

Sue could feel the knot in her stomach. "Because, Darci, I … I … don't think God would have me."

"Why would you say that, Sue? You know that Je—"

"Because my dad has sexually abused me since I was 13 and I can't stop him! What is wrong with me, Darci? I'm a very messed-up person, and no one knows. I just can't tell anyone—my mother, the police. If this all came out, it would wreck my family. What can I do?"

For once, Darci didn't know what to say.

"So *now* where's your Jesus, Darci?" Sue continued. "This is why I've always

said that God is great for people like you with wonderful lives. But he can't help people like me."

Darci finally found her voice. "No, Sue, that's not true. It's just that—"

"Never mind, Darci," Sue said. "You don't know what to do with someone as messed up as me." She turned and left.

Confused and frustrated, Darci burst into tears. *Some Christian I am,* she thought. *Abused by her dad. I actually know her parents—or at least I thought I did. God, I don't know what to say to Sue. I thought you'd be here for me when something like this happened. So where are you, God?*

The Obvious
Even disciples get in over their heads.
[Describe a time when you felt "in over your head" as a Christian.]

The Lesson
Not knowing what to do motivates us to learn what to do.
[In what areas do you need to learn more?]

The Not-So-Obvious
Jesus and everyone else gets frustrated with us when we don't "get it."
[Have you ever felt like God was frustrated with you? Describe the situation.]

The Not-So-Obvious Lesson
Jesus doesn't abandon us when he's frustrated; he teaches us.
[Do you agree or disagree with the statement above? If you agree, describe a time when you were taught by Jesus.]

for your write hand

• What did Darci's experience with Sue teach you about being a disciple?

• What would Jesus say to you right now about being incapable?

exit poll

"You know what's wrong with most Christians? They don't have enough faith. It's that simple. You want to see more miracles, then just believe more. You want to see people's lives changed, then give Jesus more of your life. There is no such thing as incapable when Jesus is around. He can do anything! And he can do anything through us, if we'd just let him."

X

INDEPENDENT

Disciple Story

Acts 15:36-40

Some time later Paul said to Barnabas, "Let us go back and visit the brothers in all the towns where we preached the word of the Lord and see how they are doing." Barnabas wanted to take John, also called Mark, with them, but Paul did not think it wise to take him, because he had deserted them in Pamphylia and had not continued with them in the work. They had such a sharp disagreement that they parted company. Barnabas took Mark and sailed for Cyprus, but Paul chose Silas and left, commended by the brothers to the grace of the Lord.

Independent though they may be, disciples are still part of a community. *Independent* means different, distinctive, unique, self-confident. Independence means you do not need to rely on others to decide what God wants you to do. It means you are not intimidated by others who feel strongly and disagree with you. Independent disciples are not shaken by disagreements or differing opinions.

Independent people recognize that many times in life we have to go a different way than others. Different doesn't mean right, it just means different. Often two people can go separate ways and both be "right." Independence is not about being right, it is about going where God wants you to go. Barnabas and Paul strongly disagreed, but they both followed God, so they just went different directions. Independence is the active part of our uniqueness. Someone said it this way: "A disciple is independently dependent on God."

Disciple Dilemma

The atmosphere was tense as Brad sat in front of his youth director's cluttered desk. "Brad, you're wasting the gifts you have. You are a great communicator, and I don't think God would give you that gift and not want you to use it."

"I know, Mike," Brad replied, "but I can write poetry, too, and that's what I really want to do. I'm good at it and I feel so alive when I'm writing it."

"Brad, feeling good is fine," Mike said, "but you have to make a living, you know. How many poets do you know who are making a living?"

"You're kidding, right?" Brad asked. "Mike, you're the one who gets up in front of youth group each week and tells us making money sucks. Now you're all worried about money."

"Brad," Mike responded. "I never said, 'Making money sucks.' I don't talk like that, for one thing. What I said was making a lot of money doesn't satisfy. But you have to eat, you have to pay for an apartment. Besides, money has nothing to do with it. You have the gift of speaking. You should go into youth ministry. You should be helping in a youth group while you're going to school. While you're doing ministry, you can write poetry in your spare time."

"Oh, sure, in my spare time," Brad said. "Look, Mike, you're a great guy. You've helped me through high school and I respect you. But when it comes to my future, you're just plain wrong. I'm not going to do youth ministry. I'm not going to college this year. I'm going to Europe. I'm going to write. I think that is what God wants me to do."

Mike looked at Brad for a few long moments before he spoke again. "Brad, I've talked to your parents. In fact, they asked me to talk to you. It's not just me—your own parents think you're making a mistake. To be honest, Brad, you're not honoring your father and mother when you refuse to listen to them."

Brad exploded inside. The whole deal was a setup. Mike had joined forces with Brad's mom and dad. Brad didn't say a word. He just stood up and walked out, knowing that if he opened his mouth he would say something very ugly. He was now 18 and old enough to make his own decisions. He wasn't disobeying his parents—he was obeying God!

The Obvious
A disciple needs to be independent as well as part of a community.
[Are you too independent or too dependent?]

The Lesson
Disciples need to learn how to disagree with each other.
[What are the skills or qualities you need to have healthy disagreements with your Christian friends?]

The Not-So-Obvious
When disciples disagree, their relationship may be broken—for a while.
[Have you ever experienced a broken relationship because of your faith?]

The Not-So-Obvious Lesson
Sometimes being a disciple can be a lonely way of life. It is part of our calling.
[How often do you feel lonely? Do you agree that loneliness is part of being a disciple? Why or why not?]

for your write hand

• What did Brad's discussion with Mike teach you about being a disciple?

• What would Jesus say to you right now about being independent?

exit poll

"Christians can't be 'lone rangers.' They have to be accountable to other Christians. Otherwise, they can become slaves to their feelings. No Christian should make a decision without the counsel and agreement of another. If you make a decision and it breaks your relationship with another Christian, then you've made the wrong decision."

MATURE

Mature is what happens when you live for awhile, have a lot of experiences (good and bad), and learn from those experiences. Maturity is not always measured by age. Young people can be mature; old people can be immature. Maturity is what causes disciples to make decisions based on deeper realities than feelings. Maturity is the opposite of impatience, worry, and anxiety.

Maturity knows how to wait. The great sign of maturity is the ability to take one's time, to refuse to act quickly, to think about options before making a decision. Maturity doesn't cancel youth out. Luckily, when you are 15 you can only be a mature 15-year-old—and that looks a lot different than a mature 50-year-old. There are levels and degrees of maturity. What characterizes disciples is not that they are all mature, but that they all desire to be more mature than they are.

disciple dilemma

Lincoln had a lot on his mind. With one month of school to go, his grades needed a boost. His dad had disappeared again and hadn't been seen for three weeks. His mom was exhausted from working two jobs. Lincoln's older brother had been arrested for drug possession and was now out on bail. Life around the house was tense. To top it all off, Lincoln was getting squeezed from his church. Lincoln had developed some friendships with guys on the football team who went to the church where "everyone" went. Lincoln was one of the few black kids who came, and as a result he got a lot of attention.

For the past six months Lincoln had been attending a small-group Bible study, and it was good. He was learning a lot about Jesus. But now Lincoln's family needed him. Even though he was the younger brother, he was going to have to take responsibility. His small-group guys were praying for him and encouraging him to stay in the Bible study no matter what, but Lincoln knew better. He needed to work on his grades and he needed to get a job to help his mom. No one at church agreed with his decision. "Look, Lincoln," they said, "our church has big bucks. We'll get some money to help your family out. You need to keep close to Jesus and keep coming to youth group." It was weird, but Lincoln knew better. Deep inside he knew he needed to help his family himself and stay close to them. He loved Jesus—that wasn't going to change—but his family needed him and he needed his family, so he made the decision to leave the small group.

Next thing you know, everyone at Lincoln's church was ragging on him, harassing him, telling him he's in danger of falling away from his faith. Instead of supporting him, people were dragging him down. Funny thing is, Lincoln feels really good about his decision. God seems even closer to Lincoln now than he did just a few weeks ago when life was much easier. Last night Lincoln fell asleep silently whispering, "Thank you, Jesus, for being here for me. You and me, God, we can do this!"

The Obvious
Each of us can become more mature.

The Lesson
Maturity doesn't just happen; it is a choice we make.

The Not-So-Obvious
Maturity is the direct result of difficult times.

The Not-So-Obvious Lesson
We learn from experience. Maturity comes from listening to our experiences.

for your write hand

• What did Lincoln's situation teach you about being a disciple?

• What would Jesus say to you right now about becoming mature?

exit poll

"Hey, nobody's mature at 17. That's the cool thing about being 17—you don't have to be mature! Why can't people let kids be kids? Why do I have behave like an adult when I'm not adult? Maturity is overrated. I don't want to be mature. I want to be immature and enjoy every minute of my life, thank you."

ORDINARY

disciple story

Acts 4:13

When they saw the courage of Peter and John and realized that they were unschooled, ordinary men, they were astonished and they took note that these men had been with Jesus.

1 Corinthians 1:26-31

Brothers, think of what you were when you were called. Not many of you were wise by human standards; not many were influential; not many were of noble birth. But God chose the foolish things of the world to shame the wise; God chose the weak things of the world to shame the strong. He chose the lowly things of this world and the despised things—and the things that are not—to nullify the things that are, so that no one may boast before him. It is because of him that you are in Christ Jesus, who has become for us wisdom from God—that is, our righteousness, holiness and redemption. Therefore, as it is written: "Let him who boasts boast in the Lord."

Ordinary means average, usual, plain, common, typical. In other words, nothing special, nothing dazzling, nothing spectacular. Just ordinary. Disciples are not known for their impressive credentials, their superior intellect, or their amazing giftedness. Disciples are just ordinary people who follow an extraordinary Lord. Disciples' power comes not from their charismatic personalities or their intellectual achievement; it comes from their powerlessness. What blows people away is how ordinary the followers of Jesus are and how much they can accomplish in their ordinariness. What also blows people away is how God chooses the ordinary. What distinguished the disciples of Jesus more than anything else—and what astonished the crowds—was how plain they were. When it comes to following Jesus, being ordinary is one of the main qualifications.

disciple dilemma

Kirsten was your basic, ordinary girl. Even though she was a junior, she had never had a date. Though many girls in her church would have been devastated to go through high school without a date, Kirsten didn't mind. She wasn't ready for all the entanglements of dating. She liked studying and reading. She liked having time to herself.

Why Kirsten decided to go with the church youth group on a summer work trip is a mystery. She had never even used a hammer before. Maybe it just sounded kind of fun to do something different. The trip to the worksite was a 10-hour drive from hell. The bus' air conditioning went out one hour into the trip. The bus itself broke down in the middle of the desert. Standing in the middle of the desert.

110 degree heat for three hours while a new bus came was not fun, but for some reason Kirsten didn't mind. She found herself energized by adversity. Most of the kids were complaining, wanting to go home, griping to the adult leaders, and generally pouting.

When the group arrived at the site five hours late, it took another three hours to set up camp in the dark. The next morning everyone was in a bad mood except Kirsten. Nobody noticed, though, because nobody ever noticed Kirsten. When they finally arrived at the building site, Kirsten found herself full of energy. She seemed to know what to do. While everyone was complaining about the heat and moping around, Kirsten was carrying wood, measuring, stacking tools, and

getting ready for the real work of the day.

Suddenly something inside Kirsten changed and she heard herself giving instructions to people. Not only was she telling kids what to do, she found herself encouraging others, bringing water to thirsty workers just when they needed it, and showing up just when someone needed help. She was amazing, and everyone began to notice. Kirsten was as surprised as anyone else. Quiet, shy Kirsten was supervising all the popular, sharp kids. It was just so out of character. Normally Kirsten never said a word. She just watched everyone else in the youth group. *Hmm,* Kirsten thought as she fell into her sleeping bag late that night, *not a bad day for a shy nerd.*

The Obvious
Disciples are just ordinary people.

[Do you believe the statement above? Why or why not?]

The Lesson
Don't try to be something you're not. Jesus likes you just the way you are.

[Does Jesus like you the way you are right now? If not, what would you have to change before he would like you?]

The Not-So-Obvious
Disciples are impressive because of their weakness, not their strength.

[Think of some of your weaknesses. Then think about why God chose you knowing you have all those weaknesses.]

The Not-So-Obvious Lesson
Disciples don't try to impress others with how cool they are. They are gratefully conscious of how ordinary they are.

[Do you really believe you are disciple material? Why or why not?]

for your write hand

• What did Kirsten's summer trip experience teach you about being a disciple?

• What would Jesus say to you right now about being ordinary?

exit poll

"God is not looking for wimpy ordinary people. Sorry, but Christians strive for excellence in everything they do. In case you haven't noticed lately, the world pays attention to winners, not losers. People want to give their lives to success, not to failure. The world listens to first place, not last place. Don't use Jesus to justify the fact that you are a loser. Give your life to Jesus so he can make you a winner."

OVERCONFIDENT

Disciple Story

Mark 14:66-72

While Peter was below in the courtyard, one of the servant girls of the high priest came by. When she saw Peter warming himself, she looked closely at him.

"You were also with that Nazarene, Jesus," she said.

But he denied it. "I don't know or understand what you're talking about," he said, and went out into the entryway.

When the servant girl saw him there, she said again to those standing around, "This fellow is one of them." Again he denied it.

After a little while, those standing near said to Peter, "Surely you are one of them, for you are a Galilean."

He began to call down curses on himself, and he swore to them, "I don't know this man you're talking about."

Immediately the rooster crowed the second time. Then Peter remembered the word Jesus had spoken to him: "Before the rooster crows twice you will disown me three times." And he broke down and wept.

Overconfident is what we all feel now and then. When life is sweet, school is great, a new girlfriend or boyfriend has just come into the picture, and everything seems under control, it's difficult not to be overconfident. Overconfidence is the feeling that nothing can go wrong, that we are invincible, strong, able to meet any challenge. A theologian by the name of C.S. Lewis said that when everything is going great we can see God everywhere. (He also said that when life is not great we can't find God anywhere.) Often when life is good we begin to take our eyes off God and start relying or depending on our own circumstances. Usually we are not aware of this shift in focus. The longer that life is good the easier it is to forget about God and rely on ourselves. Before we know it our thinking shifts from "God is so good" to "I am so cool," and *then* we are in trouble. Overconfidence tricks us into believing that nothing can derail us, defeat us, or corrupt us. But when that happens we are already corrupt. Here's the ugly truth: the only solution for overconfidence is humiliation. In other words, when you climb up a tower, the only way down is to fall. Falling off the tower of overconfidence is not fun, but more often than not it's a very effective way to get our focus back on Jesus.

Disciple Dilemma

Tito sat in front of the stadium with the other graduates and smiled. Life was good. The last few years had been especially tough in the barrio. His brother was in jail...his sister had been in and out of drugs but was finally doing better. The rock of the family was Tito, the one his mom and dad were very proud of, the first in his family to graduate from high school. He'd be the first child to attend college. The scholarship had come in and his job was looking good for the summer. Tito knew that his strength had come from God. Since he had become a Christian, his life had turned around. His youth director had always helped, but this year God had stepped in big-time. Tito had kept his grades up and stayed out of trouble, and now he was reaping the rewards. Life was good.

It had even been a year since he had been in a fight. His temper still flared now and then, but with God in his life he knew his fighting days were over. After graduation Tito drove to meet his friends at McDonald's for lunch and a final celebration of a great year. On the way to McDonald's, rap music maxed out on his low-rider stereo, he was pulled over by a cop.

"Out of the car and hands on the roof! *Now!*"

Tito was taken by surprise. He could feel the anger flare inside of him. *Come on*, he thought. *Stay calm. Jesus, I need your help.*

He spoke to the cop as evenly as he could. "Hey, what's the problem, man? What'd I do?"

"I don't need to tell you anything, Mexican man, except there's been a robbery and you look like the person who did it. Now out of the car."

Tito's anger was building. "Excuse me, sir, but I don't like being called 'Mexican man' and I was just at my graduation. I have lots of witnesses."

"Listen, *Mexican man*, I don't have time to mess with you. Get out of the car and do as I say!"

Tito lost it. "You can take your damn badge and shove it, *pig!*"

Thirty minutes later Tito, still furious, sat waiting at juvenile hall to be picked up by his parents. The P.D. had apologized for the mistake. But Tito was mad at God for letting this happen—and mad at himself for losing his temper. Apparently his faith wasn't as life-changing as he thought it was.

The Obvious
Overconfidence can happen to any of us.
[When was the last time you felt overconfident?]

The Lesson
Always be on the alert.
[What are some practical things you can do to keep from getting overconfident?]

The Not-So-Obvious
Genuine tears over genuine sin is the beginning of growth.
[When was the last time you cried over a failure in your life?]

The Not-So-Obvious Lesson
It is not the absence of sin that distinguishes true disciples, it is the sadness over our sin.
[If you were to look up and see Jesus standing in front of you with tears in his eyes, what aspect of your life do you suppose would be causing his tears?]

for your write hand

• What did Tito's encounter with the police officer teach you about overconfidence?

• What would Jesus say to you right now about overconfidence?

exit poll

"How can you be overconfident if you're a Christian? I mean, Christians are supposed to have a big faith. I can hardly open my Bible without reading stuff like 'You have not because you ask not' and 'I can do everything through Christ.' All I know is, in the same year my dad finally got a job, and God healed him of cancer. if I hadn't been 'overconfident' and prayed like God could do the impossible, I don't think he would've."

PRACTICAL

Disciple Story

John 6:5-13

When Jesus looked up and saw a great crowd coming toward him, he said to Philip, "Where shall we buy bread for these people to eat?" He asked this only to test him, for he already had in mind what he was going to do.

Philip answered him, "Eight months wages would not buy enough bread for each one to have a bite!"

Another of his disciples, Andrew, Simon Peter's brother, spoke up, "Here is a boy with five small barley loaves and two small fish, but how far will they go among so many?"

Jesus said, "Have the people sit down." There was plenty of grass in that place, and the men sat down, about five thousand of them. Jesus then took the loaves, gave thanks, and distributed to those who were seated as much as they wanted. He did the same with the fish.

When they had all had enough to eat, he said to his disciples, "Gather the pieces that are left over. Let nothing be wasted." So they gathered them and filled twelve baskets with the pieces of the five barley loaves left over by those who had eaten.

Practical means down-to-earth, sensible, realistic. People who are practical are simple, focused, and able to see what lies before them. A practical person says, "I could get my term paper done the night before it's due, but if anything goes wrong, I'm dead. If my computer crashes, if the power goes out, if I run out of paper at three in the morning, my assignment is doomed. So I'll start working on it a month in advance." A practical person says, "I might have enough will power to say no to sex if I watch videos at my girlfriend's house with her parents gone for the weekend, but I probably won't, so we'd better go someplace else." Practical people give God what they have instead of complaining about what they don't have. Practical people believe "something is better than nothing." Practical people don't sit back and ask God to do everything while they do nothing. Instead they do something and then ask God to bless that something. Practical disciples give God what they can and assume God will bless their gift.

Disciple Dilemma

"If God really wants us to go to Ecuador for three months of discipleship training and missions work in Ecuador, we'll raise the $18,000," Brad said confidently. He and his two best friends in the youth group were looking forward to their last summer together before heading off to college, and they wanted to spend it this way. They decided to graduate early, take three months to raise their support, and head to Ecuador the first day of summer. All they needed to do, they figured, was make a presentation at church, send support letters to their family and friends, and then watch God answer prayer. They were confident God would provide. The church had already committed $6,000, and the guys just knew the other $12,000 would come in.

Since they were so sure God wanted them to go to Ecuador, they opted against working during the months preceding their trip. Instead they spent three months camping, hiking, boating, hanging out at the beach. Two weeks before their departure date, the boys counted up the pledges of support—and couldn't believe the numbers. They had raised less than $12,000—$6,000 short of the amount they needed. What had gone wrong? How could they have been so sure of God's leading and not get the support they needed? Disappointed, angry with God, and now in a dilemma, they called their youth director.

"Sure, I think God wants you guys to go to Ecuador," Trina told them, "but you've blown it big time."

"What do you mean?" they asked. "We've contacted everyone we could think of!"

"I know. But if each of you had gotten a full-time job for the three months you've been out of school, you would have ended up with just enough. Instead you decided to play around these last few weeks—and now it's too late."

The guys hung up the phone angry. "This is totally stupid," they agreed. "If God wanted us to go to Ecuador, he would have come through. He understands how important our friendship is." The guys talked a long time that night, and finally decided that God *didn't* want them to go to Ecuador that summer. So they returned the money and pledges, got part-time jobs at fast-food places at the beach, and spent the summer working on their friendship and their tans.

The Obvious

Jesus didn't make something out of nothing, he made something out of something.

[Pretend you're the little boy with the loaves and fishes and Andrew has brought you to Jesus. What would you be thinking?]

The Lesson

Don't expect God to do what you can do.

[List a problem in your life. Then list what you can do about the problem and what God can do.*]

The Not-So-Obvious

Jesus was testing his disciples.

[Have you ever felt like you were being tested by God?]

The Not-So-Obvious Lesson

We need tests to know how we're growing.

[Maybe God isn't deliberately sending tests your way, but maybe he is. What do you think? Does God test us?]

for your write hand

• What did Brad, Dan, and Reggie's experience teach you about being practical?

• What would Jesus say to you right now about how practical you are?

exit poll

"Basically God leaves us alone. Oh, he loves us all right and cares about us, but he doesn't intervene or get involved. He leaves our lives up to us. So, of course, we have to be practical because God isn't going to step in and do anything. If work gets done for Jesus, it's up to us to do it."

*Here's an example:

Problem: Brother is involved in drugs. What you can do: Pray. Leave him a note each night telling him how much I love him and worry about him. Clean his room without saying anything. What God can do: Make him receptive to our family's concern and love. Keep him from harming himself.

PREPARED

disciple story

Luke 14:28-35

"Suppose one of you wants to build a tower. Will he not first sit down and estimate the cost to see if he has enough money to complete it? For if he lays the foundation and is not able to finish it, everyone who sees it will ridicule him, saying, 'This fellow began to build and was not able to finish.'

"Or suppose a king is about to go to war against another king. Will he not first sit down and consider whether he is able with ten thousand men to oppose the one coming against him with twenty thousand? If he is not able, he will send a delegation while the other is still a long way off and will ask for terms of peace. In the same way, any of you who does not give up everything he has cannot be my disciple.

"Salt is good, but if it loses its saltiness, how can it be made salty again? It is fit neither for the soil nor for the manure pile; it is thrown out.

"He who has ears to hear, let him hear."

Prepared means being ready. Preparation is not a guarantee of success, but it is a guarantee against being surprised. When the unexpected happens, because of your faith in Christ, it is not really unexpected. When you are prepared, you expect things to happen. You may not know *what* or *when* something is going to happen, but you know in your gut there is more to come. When you are a prepared disciple, you know being a disciple will be costly. You understand that following Jesus could cost you relationships, your reputation, and—well, not just everything, but anything. Following Jesus is not a slam dunk! It's hard and expensive. Good disciples understand how costly their faith will be.

disciple dilemma

Before he became a Christian, Don had been sexually involved with all of his girlfriends. Then he met Leslie at church. It had been difficult, but Don held the line on sexual activity—with some help from his youth director, who explained to him that being a Christian wasn't easy, and to look out for one's weakness. Don's weakness was sex. He wasn't proud of his sexual experiences, but they stayed with him and made it really difficult for him to *not* get sexually involved with Leslie. The couple had been dating for a year now, and there had been no slip-ups. Don was starting to believe his commitment to Christ was taking hold.

That's why Leslie's note blindsided him. For a half hour he just sat on his bed, staring at the note, reading and rereading it. When he dropped her off at work that day, she said, "Oh, Don, I left you a note in your backpack. Don't read it until you get home." Their one-year anniversary was the next day, so Don expected a very hot letter. Instead he got this:

Dear Don,

From the very beginning of our relationship I knew you were special. I loved you from the first time we started talking in English. I'd seen you at church a lot, but never really talked to you. When we finally connected I thought this would be forever. I know you love me, Don, and I love you, too. But I guess I've come to the conclusion I'm not the girl for you. I mean, I don't think I'm good enough for you. See, Don, I've always had a sexual relationship with the guys I've gone steady with, and from the beginning you made it clear you didn't want that with us. At first I thought that was the coolest thing. Secretly, I guess, I believed we would not have sex for awhile, but once we knew we loved each other we would give in to it. But you haven't given in, and I can't believe I'm saying this, but it bothers me. I want more from a guy than just going places and talking. I want to feel like he wants me, all of me. I guess I want what sex gives more than I thought. So, Don, I really respect you and think you are cool, but I just don't think I'm good for you. I know this is news to you, but I've been thinking about it for a long time and I've actually been seeing another guy for awhile. I know this must hurt you, Don, but I'm sure God will help you find the right girl. I'm just not her.

The Obvious
Genuine faith is never easy.
[What is the most difficult experience you've had because of your faith?]

The Lesson
The more you read the Bible, the better prepared you will be.
[What is your favorite part of the Bible to read? Why? What's your least favorite? Why?]

The Not-So-Obvious
Being prepared is knowing you're not prepared.
[Put this statement in your own words.]

The Not-So-Obvious Lesson
Preparation doesn't guarantee success.
[Ever have a time in your life when you thought you were prepared for what would happen to you as a Christian, but weren't? What happened?]

for your write hand

• What did Leslie's breakup with Don teach you about being prepared?

• What would Jesus say to you right now about being prepared?

exit poll

"You know what, I'm ready. Yeah, I'm ready for anything Satan wants to throw at me. All these people who say you never know what's going to happen. Maybe so, but I don't have to know. I only have to know Jesus, and I do. I'm prayed up and Bible'd up. There's nothing Satan could do to me to cause me to waver in my faith. I'm hard-core-trust-Jesus-to-the-end, and nothing's gonna change that. Trust me, I'm prepared."

SEEKING

Disciple Story

John 1:35-42

The next day John was there again with two of his disciples. When he saw Jesus passing by, he said, "Look, the Lamb of God!"

When the two disciples heard him say this, they followed Jesus. Turning around, Jesus saw them following and asked, "What do you want?"

They said, "Rabbi!" (which means Teacher), "where are you staying?"

"Come," he replied, "and you will see."

So they went and saw where he was staying, and spent that day with him. It was about the tenth hour.

Andrew, Simon Peter's brother, was one of the two who heard what John had said and who had followed Jesus. The first thing Andrew did was to find his brother Simon and tell him, "We have found the Messiah" (that is, the Christ). Then he brought Simon to Jesus, who looked at him and said, "You are Simon son of John. You will be called Cephas" (which, when translated, is Peter).

Seeking is searching, probing, stalking. Seekers aren't satisfied with secondhand experience. They want to see, to touch, to taste, to know with all their senses what they are looking for. Seekers don't give up easily. They are persistent, unrelenting, fearless, and focused. In the case of John's disciples, they were seeking the Messiah. John had talked about him and had identified Jesus as him. Suddenly the men who were disciples of John became disciples of Jesus. Their seeking caused them to follow Jesus, hang out with him, talk with him, and get to know him. It's interesting that the John who recorded the Bible passage above about the disciples' beginning with Jesus, wrote toward the end of his life, "That which was from the beginning, which we have heard, which we have seen with our eyes, which we have looked at and our hands have touched—this we proclaim...." (1 John 1:1). Seekers settle for nothing less than the real thing. Seekers seek with their whole selves. And one other thing: true seekers find.

Disciple Dilemma

Ever since I became a Christian my life has been miserable. Here's the deal: a friend of mine brought me to a concert at his church. My folks were divorced when I was 13 and, to be honest, I've never quite recovered. I live with my mom and I love her a lot, but I do miss my dad, even though he ran off and married his secretary—but that's another story. So I go to this concert, which was really cool, and the lead singer talks about how he used to be on drugs and stuff, how his parents were all screwed up, and how he met Jesus and had his life turned around. Then he asked if anyone wanted to know Jesus like he did, and I said, "Yes!"

I had no idea what trouble my faith was going to cause! I had a million questions. On the way home from the concert I was going crazy with questions. All my friends were excited that I had become a Christian, but they were totally clueless about my questions. They told me to talk to the youth director. The next day I did, and I still am. But I can tell he doesn't want to talk to me anymore. And I can tell that all the kids in the youth group are sick of my questions. I raise my hand and I can hear everyone groan.

So I've stopped asking questions. It's killing me, but everyone's much more relaxed. They actually like being around me, which should make me feel great, but doesn't. My questions are eating at me and I'm beginning to wonder if this Jesus stuff is for real. How come no one else has my questions? How come none of my friends are as excited about Jesus as I am? Don't get me wrong, I'm not thinking I'm some cool Christian. I just feel like I'm some kind of freak. Am I? See what I mean? I still can't stop asking questions.

The Obvious
A disciple is a person who never stops seeking.
[When you go to be with God what are the top three questions you would ask him?]

The Lesson
Don't let anyone or anything keep you from seeking God.
[What obstacles, if any, are keeping you from seeking God right now?]

The Not-So-Obvious
Seeking isn't about getting answers; it's about never giving up.
[Put this statement in your own words.]

The Not-So-Obvious Lesson
Don't give up seeking or your faith will wither and die.
[Sometime today, write God a letter expressing your desire to know him better, to know more about him.]

for your write hand

• What did the disciple dilemma teach you about being a disciple?

• What would Jesus say to you right now about seeking?

exit poll

"Tonight our youth leader said we're supposed to have questions and seek after God. Great! Now I have something else to feel guilty about. I don't have any questions. I can't even think of any. I believe in God. I believe in Jesus. I believe in the Bible. I'm just trying to do what Jesus says, not sit around and think of stupid questions to ask."

SENSITIVE

disciple story

Mark 5:24-34

A large crowd followed and pressed around him. And a woman was there who had been subject to bleeding for twelve years. She had suffered a great deal under the care of many doctors and had spent all she had, yet instead of getting better she grew worse. When she heard about Jesus, she came up behind him in the crowd and touched his cloak, because she thought, "If I just touch his clothes, I will be healed." Immediately her bleeding stopped and she felt in her body that she was freed from her suffering.

At once Jesus realized that power had gone out from him. He turned around in the crowd and asked, "Who touched my clothes?"

"You see the people crowding against you," his disciples answered, "and yet you can ask, 'Who touched me?'"

But Jesus kept looking around to see who had done it. Then the woman, knowing what had happened to her, came and fell at his feet and, trembling with fear, told him the whole truth. He said to her, "Daughter, your faith has healed you. Go in peace and be freed from your suffering."

Sensitive means you're aware of others. You can see what's going on *inside*, not just outside. You can interpret body language as well as spoken language. A sensitive person looks into other people's eyes and can tell if they're upset, if they're being honest, if they're holding something back, if they're angry. Sensitive people are observant, but gentle. They don't try to expose others, but rather support them, encourage them, *be* with them. Being a Christian doesn't give a person the right to preach to others about their needs or to immediately try to fix those needs. A real disciple notices the need first, works to understand that need, and *then* decides what to do. Disciples don't exist to fix people, but to *notice* people.

disciple dilemma

Last night at church my youth worker said, "If you are serious about being a disciple, then you need to care about other people. So why not have lunch with a loner or show attention to someone everyone else ignores?" So I did.

Big mistake. I had lunch with this loner guy, and now he follows me around everywhere I go. There's a reason why he's a loner, and now I want him to go back to being a loner. Oh, and get this: I hung around after class to walk this very overweight girl to her next class, trying to be nice to her. Now guess who wants to be my next girlfriend. My friends are having a lot of laughs at my expense. I don't mind helping the needy, but I don't want to be their lifetime buddy.

The Obvious
The disciples completely overlooked the needy woman.
[Think about your friends and the students at school. Who are the needy ones? Not necessarily poor, but simply those who need your sensitivity in some way?]

The Lesson
Disciples want to be good followers and good noticers.
[What are some ways you can notice the needs of your "needy" friends and acquaintances?]

The Not-So-Obvious
A disciple can be close to Jesus and still miss the needs of others.
[How would you define close to Jesus?]

The Not-So-Obvious Lesson
A good gauge of how close you are to Jesus is how sensitive you are to others' needs.
[Where are you on this scale?]

Not Sensitive _____ Too Sensitive

for your write hand

• What did the disciple dilemma teach you about being a disciple?

• When was the last time you felt sensitive?

• What would Jesus say to you right now about your sensitivity?

exit poll

"Not all disciples have to be sensitive. Girls and gay guys may be, but most guys don't do sensitive."

X

SERVANT-LIKE

Disciple Story

John 13:2, 4-5, 12-17

The evening meal was being served . . . so he got up from the meal, took off his outer clothing, and wrapped a towel around his waist. After that, he poured water into a basin and began to wash his disciples' feet, drying them with the towel that was wrapped around him. . . .

When he had finished washing their feet, he put on his clothes and returned to his place. "Do you understand what I have done for you?" he asked them. "You call me 'Teacher' and 'Lord,' and rightly so, for that is what I am. Now that I, your Lord and Teacher, have washed your feet, you also should wash one another's feet. I have set you an example that you should do as I have done for you. I tell you the truth, no servant is greater than his master, nor is a messenger greater than the one who sent him. Now that you know these things, you will be blessed if you do them."

Servant-like persons care for others. Servants actively look for ways to help others by listening, watching, and paying attention. Servants are sensitive. They can tell when someone is hurting or in need. Servants know how to help others so that the one being helped does not feel demeaned or used. Serving is done for the benefit of others, not for the benefit of one's self. Servanthood is not a one-time experience; it's a way of life—one that takes a lifetime to learn. You don't become Mother Teresa in a week. True servanthood becomes more possible the more we hang out with Jesus, read about him, think about him, and talk about him. Jesus set the example. He not only washed the disciples' feet, he gave his life for them.

By the way, servanthood is also hard. And humiliating. And awkward. And difficult. But it's also blessed when you do it. Jesus said so.

Disciple Dilemma

What the heck, Craig thought—I've never spent a day with Down Syndrome kids before. His youth pastor had talked him into helping at the Special Olympics, and soon he was introduced to Ellie. Craig took a liking to her immediately and took it upon himself to be her personal servant all day.

The day started well, but went downhill fast. Ellie became more difficult and tiring. Craig could understand Ellie's conversation only with difficulty. After one race and then two, she became stubborn, rude, and just plain irritating to Craig. Just one more race, Craig thought.

Ellie finally agreed and did fine—until about halfway through the 200-meter race, when she suddenly stopped running. Other runners stopped, grabbed her hand, and tried to get her to run with them. Ellie refused, and the runners finally went on.

Craig was fed up with Ellie now. "Ellie! Stop being a jerk and whining!" he yelled as he trotted across the track to her. "You signed up for the race, and you're going to finish it!"

Ellie looked at him and Craig could see her eyes well with tears. "Cwaig, I...I...don't feel so gwood." And before Craig could dodge, right there she vomited all over the front of him.

Oh yeah, servanthood is great, Craig thought on his drive home (with windows wide open in a vain attempt to rid the car of the stench). You try to help people who don't want your help, they won't cooperate, and then throw up all over you.

Thirty minutes later, on his way out of the shower, he heard the phone chirp and picked it up.

"Craig? This is Don Sykes, Ellie's dad. (Oh great, Craig thought, now I'm going to get a lecture from him.)

She wants to talk to you."

Before Craig could react, Ellie was on the phone, sniffly and weepy. "Uh, Cwaig, I want to thank you for helping me today. Nobwody ever do that for me. I'm sworry I wasn't bery nice. I didn't feel gwood. But I guess you know I wasn't fweeling gwood. I throw up on you. I...I sworry, Cwaig."

Craig swallowed hard. "It's okay, Ellie. I'm sorry for getting so mad at you."

"Oh, it's okay, Cwaig," Ellie said. "I forgwive you. Lots of people get mad at me, but you didn't get mad like they do. Would . . . would you be my fwiend?"

The lump in Craig's throat began showing in his eyes. "Sure, Ellie. I'd love to be your friend."

And with that news, Ellie actually giggled. "Oh, goodie," she said. "You know what Cwaig? I ownwy throw up on my fwiends."

The Obvious
Part of being a disciple is serving others.
[When was the last time you served someone else?]

The Lesson
Service is a choice, not something you do automatically.
[How often are you involved in service? Once a day? Once a week? Once a month? Once a year? Do you believe you are involved in enough service?]

The Not-So-Obvious
Service always takes a toll on the server.
[What happened to you personally the last time you served someone?]

The Not-So-Obvious Lesson
Serving can be hard and scary, but also very rewarding.
[Think of someone you don't know personally who you can serve today.]

for your write hand

• What did Craig's adventure with Ellie teach you about being a disciple?

• What would Jesus say to you right now about your service?

exit poll

"Sure, I think service is important, but only if you choose to do it. I don't think it should be a requirement for being a disciple. I don't serve much, and I know a lot of other folks who don't, either. Don't try to make me feel guilty for not serving enough."

SHREWD

disciple story

Luke 16:1-9

There was a rich man whose manager was accused of wasting his possessions. So he called him in and asked him, "What is this I hear about you? Give an account of your management, because you cannot be manager any longer."

The manager said to himself, "What shall I do now? My master is taking away my job. I'm not strong enough to dig, and I'm ashamed to beg—I know what I'll do so that, when I lose my job here, people will welcome me into their houses."

So he called in each one of his master's debtors. He asked the first, "How much do you owe my master?"

"Eight hundred gallons of olive oil," he replied. The manager told him, "Take your bill, sit down quickly, and make it four hundred." Then he asked the second, "And how much do you owe?"

"A thousand bushels of wheat," he replied. He told him, "Take your bill and make it eight hundred." The master commended the dishonest manager because he had acted shrewdly. For the people of this world are more shrewd in dealing with their own kind than are the people of the light. I tell you, use worldly wealth to gain friends for yourselves, so that when it is gone, you will be welcomed into eternal dwellings.

Shrewd is a word you don't hear much among Christians, probably because it has a sneaky, devious, shifty sound to it. Yet Jesus suggested that shrewdness is a good thing. So what's he talking about, anyway? Try saying *street smart* instead of *shrewd*. Maybe Jesus is saying that Christians need to know the neighborhood, need to know how to navigate their way through a sneaky, devious, shifty world. Street-smart people aren't evil—they're survivors. They know where to go and where *not* to go if they want to stay alive.

Lots of times Jesus asked the Pharisees questions he knew they couldn't answer publicly. Frankly, Jesus set 'em up *exactly so* they couldn't answer him without getting in trouble with the crowds. Being a disciple is not only about following Jesus—it's about using your brain, keeping your eyes open, and being tough when you need to be (and *only* when you need to be). Being shrewd means following Jesus with your heart and with your street smarts.

disciple dilemma

Danielle was angry with her church. The congregation had decided to spend three million dollars to build a new "Family Life Center," a "safe, pleasant atmosphere for families to be together." Danielle may have been only 16, but she knew what the phrase meant. It meant the church people didn't want to use public facilities for racquetball, swimming, and working out. It meant the church people didn't want to be "contaminated" by non-Christians.

Danielle had complained to her parents, her youth minister, and her pastor to no avail. "Three million dollars could go a long way in Haiti or Africa," she protested. All she received in return was a pat on the head and words like "That's a wonderful idea, Danielle, but our church already gives to missions."

So Danielle spread the word to the youth group. The plan was to have them show up at the annual business meeting where the congregation was going to vote on the Family Life Center, and challenge the church: "We, the young people, challenge the congregation to match the money spent on the Family Life Center and use it for world hunger."

More than a hundred young people showed up, each with a poster that read "Our families live while other families are dying." Danielle had called the newspaper and a local TV station to tell them of her plan. What a meeting! Before cameras and microphones, she said, "We're not against the Family Life Center, but we are against our families living while other families are dying. We are willing to give up our entire youth budget so that families around the world can live. All we're asking is that for every one dollar the church spends on the Family Life Center, it matches that dollar by spending it on world hunger."

Two years later, the church has its Family Life Center—and has raised three million dollars for hunger relief around the world.

The Obvious
Disciples are streetwise.
[What does streetwise mean to you?]

The Lesson
It is just as important to think about what you're doing as it is to pray about what you're doing.
[Do you agree or disagree with the statement above? Why or why not?]

The Not-So-Obvious
Outsmarting people can make them mad.
[Have you ever experienced a situation in which your faith made someone mad?]

The Not-So-Obvious Lesson
Good disciples have friends and enemies.
[What enemies do you have because of your faith in Christ?]

for your write hand

• What did Danielle's actions teach you about being a disciple?

• What would Jesus say to you right now about being shrewd?

exit poll

"Christians don't try to outsmart people. They don't try to win arguments and make others look stupid. Christians aren't street smart, they're humble and powerless. We don't fight the enemy, we pray for our enemies while they are persecuting us. This shrewd stuff is not Christian—it's just wrong, period."

STRONG

disciple story

John 6:60, 66-69

On hearing it, many of his disciples said, "This is a hard teaching. Who can accept it?" . . .

From this time many of his disciples turned back and no longer followed him.

"You do not want to leave too, do you?" Jesus asked the Twelve.

Simon Peter answered him, "Lord, to whom shall we go? You have the words of eternal life. We believe and know that you are the Holy One of God."

Strong, stable, durable, impregnable, rugged, passionate, intense, constant—all of these are different ways of saying the same thing. Admit it—there are moments, days, weeks, even months when you feel strong, passionate, and zealous. That's good. During our strong moments we feel invincible, impregnable, and powerful—like nothing can defeat us or get us down. When we feel strong, there is nothing like it. It's a "mountaintop moment" when no one can cause us to weaken or stumble.

Yet no matter how strong we feel, weakness is always just a moment away. Read the passage above again. Notice that Peter is the strong one. Yet he is just a few months away from being the weak one. Feeling strong can trick us into believing we will never be weak. Good disciples understand that strength never stays with us, so we must always be prepared for the weakness that is as much a part of being a disciple as strength is. We must always remember our strength is not in our feelings, but in Jesus who is our strength even when we feel weak (1 Corinthians 1:25).

disciple dilemma

Logan was blown away. She had never experienced the nearness of God like she had at camp. She had never been able to stand in front of a group of kids and say anything, even at school. Not only was she shy, but crowds made her very nervous. But there she was, standing in front of 50 kids, telling them about Jesus and what he meant to her. What's weird is that she wasn't afraid, and with every word she felt stronger and bolder. Watching her friends stare at her in amazement gave her even more confidence.

There was no doubt in Logan's mind that this Jesus stuff was real. It had changed her life, and she wanted everyone to know about it.

Earlier in the evening she had called her parents to tell them she was going to stand up at campfire and tell the kids about her relationship with Jesus. She could tell her parents were pleasantly shocked. She could hear it in their voices. They kept asking her if she was all right. She thought to herself, *All right? I'm more right than I've ever been.* She went to sleep that night feeling like a new person, just like the Bible said.

However, a week after camp, Logan found her old fears coming back. She had decided to talk about her faith in Christ as part of a report for English class on her goals in life. The night before the report was due, Logan felt very afraid. *I can't*

do this, she thought. *Everyone will think I'm crazy. Maybe I am. I can't talk about Jesus in front of my English class. Come on, God, where are you? Help me to be strong. I can do this and I know you can help me.*

The next morning Logan woke up nauseated and weak. When she threw up her dinner from the night before, Logan's parents decided she had better stay home. She felt relieved until the guilt hit her: *Great, Logan, you really are a strong Christian, all right. You can't even keep your dinner down. Face it, you were just all emotional at camp, that's all. Now it's back to the real world."*

The Obvious

When you're strong, you are strong.

[List the moments in the past few days (or weeks) when you have felt strong.]

The Lesson

Being strong is great. Enjoy it—it's real!

[Describe what it feels like to be gung-ho for God.]

The Not-So-Obvious

When you're weak, Jesus is strong.

[Put the statement above in your own words.]

The Not-So-Obvious Lesson

God's strength is with you all the time.

[Can you think of a time when you were bummed out and God showed up in some way?]

for your write hand

• What did Logan's short-lived strength teach you about being a disciple?

• What would Jesus say to you right now about being strong?

exit poll

"Look, the goal of every Christian should be to get strong. Just like people who go to the gym and exercise every day to stay strong, so Christians can go to God's word every day to stay strong. Once you're strong, you don't have to give in to weakness. People who say weakness is always a possibility are wimps. I am not going to be a wimp for Jesus. I'm going to be strong for Jesus, and that's what every Christian should strive for."

X

WEAK

Matthew 26:36, 38-41

Then Jesus went with his disciples to a place called Gethsemane, and he said to them, "Sit here while I go over there and pray." Then he said to them, "My soul is overwhelmed with sorrow to the point of death. Stay here and keep watch with me."

Going a little farther, he fell with his face to the ground and prayed.... Then he returned to his disciples and found them sleeping. "Could you men not keep watch with me for one hour?" he asked Peter. "Watch and pray so that you will not fall into temptation. The spirit is willing, but the body is weak."

Weak is a word that reminds us of an unfortunate truth: humans are not strong. Christians or non-Christians, young or old, healthy or sick—it doesn't matter. Weakness is a fact of life for everyone, whether it's a weakness caused by disease, by emotional problems, by not taking care of yourself. Then there are natural weaknesses—like needing to eat, to exercise, to drink fluids, to sleep. No matter how dedicated a Christian you are, you have to take care of these natural needs.

It's important that you understand your weaknesses and not deny them. The limitations of your body affect the rest of your life. If you're deprived of sleep, drink, exercise, or food, you're susceptible to illness, irritation, bad judgment, and faulty thinking. In other words, you tend to make dumb mistakes and bad decisions. Disciples may have spiritual motivations and goals, but they have bodily needs. If you don't pay attention to your physical weaknesses, then you end up missing opportunities. The sleeping disciples didn't sin—but they *did* miss out helping their Lord at a critical time. (And imagine how many times after Jesus died those disciples wished they could have relived that dark night.)

DISCIPLE DILEMMA

Kristin didn't want to get out of bed. Her entire body ached. She was sick to her stomach and it seemed as though every part of her was in pain. How could last night have happened? Kristin had never been more miserable. She felt embarrassed, humiliated, angry, disgusted, guilty, hurt, and disappointed.

Kristin had been going to Bible study every week. She woke up every morning one hour early to pray and read her Bible. Not only was she in a small group that met once a week, she had recently begun meeting in an "accountability group" with Cheryl and Grace. The members of the group were supposed to keep each other accountable and ask for support when they were in trouble. But Kristin doubted that she would ever be able to admit what had happened.

It was finals week and Kristin had been studying late every night. She figured she had slept about eight hours total for the whole week. The night after her last final she decided to celebrate with her boyfriend Kenny. They were going to a movie and then to Veggies, a new restaurant for vegetarians, for a late-night snack. Just as she and Kenny were leaving her house, Kristin's mom called. "I . . . uh . . . have to work late, Kristin. Don't wait up for me." Kristin knew what her mom meant. Her mom had been married three times and seemed to have a new boyfriend every other week. She usually ended up sleeping with her boyfriends and sneaking in at about four in the morning. Kristin's mother was a pathetic example of a parent.

Kristin could feel the anger inside. "Fine, Mom, whatever," she said and hung up. She was so angry she said to Kenny, "Let's just go to your place and rent a video. I don't feel like going out."

Kenny agreed very enthusiastically, "Sure. My folks are gone for a couple of days, anyway."

Kristin normally would have said no, but tonight she just didn't care. No parents, no sleep, no mom, and one beer, and the next thing Kristin knew she and Kenny were almost close to having sex. Somehow she was able to pull herself away, pull her clothes back on, and get out of the house—but she had violated every Christian value she had. Some disciple she was.

The Obvious
The disciples were too tired to do what Jesus asked.
[When was the last time you were too tired to "hang in there" with God?]

The Lesson
Disciples need to take care of their soul and their body.
[What bodily or physical weaknesses do you have? Do you find them getting in the way of your faith?]

The Not-So-Obvious
Getting plenty of sleep is good discipleship.
[How exhausted are you? Mark the exhaustion meter.]

Totally Exhausted

Totally Rested

The Not-So-Obvious Lesson
There are times when taking a nap or eating a meal is more spiritual than reading your Bible or praying.

for your write hand

• What did Kristin's experience teach you about being a disciple?

• What would Jesus say to you right now about your weaknesses?

exit poll

"My youth director says Jesus is coming soon and we need to tell everyone we can about the gospel before it's too late. How can I rest or take time off when the stakes are so high? It doesn't matter whether I get enough sleep. Christians should be exhausted all the time because they are so concerned with reaching the world for Jesus."

X

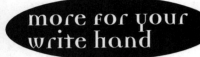
more for your
write hand

more for your
write hand

WWJD

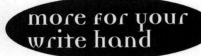
more for your
write hand

RESOURCES FROM YOUTH SPECIALTIES

Professional Resources
Administration, Publicity, & Fundraising (Ideas Library)
Developing Student Leaders
Equipped to Serve: Volunteer Youth Worker Training Course
Help! I'm a Junior High Youth Worker!
Help! I'm a Small-Group Leader!
Help! I'm a Sunday School Teacher!
Help! I'm a Volunteer Youth Worker!
How to Expand Your Youth Ministry
How to Speak to Youth...and Keep Them Awake at the Same Time
Junior High Ministry (Updated & Expanded)
The Ministry of Nurture: A Youth Worker's Guide to Discipling Teenagers
One Kid at a Time: Reaching Youth through Mentoring
Purpose-Driven Youth Ministry
So *That's* Why I Keep Doing This! 52 Devotional Stories for Youth Workers
A Youth Ministry Crash Course
The Youth Worker's Handbook to Family Ministry

Youth Ministry Programming
Camps, Retreats, Missions, & Service Ideas (Ideas Library)
Compassionate Kids: Practical Ways to Involve Your Students in Mission and Service
Creative Bible Lessons from the Old Testament
Creative Bible Lessons in John: Encounters with Jesus
Creative Bible Lessons in Romans: Faith on Fire!
Creative Bible Lessons on the Life of Christ
Creative Junior High Programs from A to Z, Vol. 1 (A-M)
Creative Junior High Programs from A to Z, Vol. 2 (N-Z)
Creative Meetings, Bible Lessons, & Worship Ideas (Ideas Library)
Crowd Breakers & Mixers (Ideas Library)
Drama, Skits, & Sketches (Ideas Library)
Drama, Skits, & Sketches 2 (Ideas Library)

Dramatic Pauses
Everyday Object Lessons
Facing Your Future: Graduating Youth Group with a Faith That Lasts
Games (Ideas Library)
Games 2 (Ideas Library)
Great Fundraising Ideas for Youth Groups
More Great Fundraising Ideas for Youth Groups
Great Retreats for Youth Groups
Greatest Skits on Earth
Greatest Skits on Earth, Vol. 2
Holiday Ideas (Ideas Library)
Hot Illustrations for Youth Talks
More Hot Illustrations for Youth Talks
Still More Hot Illustrations for Youth Talks
Incredible Questionnaires for Youth Ministry
Junior High Game Nights
More Junior High Game Nights
Kickstarters: 101 Ingenious Intros to Just about Any Bible Lesson
Live the Life! Student Evangelism Training Kit
Memory Makers
Play It! Great Games for Groups
Play It Again! More Great Games for Groups
Special Events (Ideas Library)
Spontaneous Melodramas
Super Sketches for Youth Ministry
Teaching the Bible Creatively
What Would Jesus Do? Youth Leader's Kit
WWJD—The Next Level
Wild Truth Bible Lessons
Wild Truth Bible Lessons 2
Worship Services for Youth Groups

Discussion Starters
Discussion & Lesson Starters (Ideas Library)
Discussion & Lesson Starters 2 (Ideas Library)
Get 'Em Talking
Keep 'Em Talking!
High School TalkSheets
More High School TalkSheets
High School TalkSheets: Psalms and Proverbs
Junior High TalkSheets
More Junior High TalkSheets

Junior High TalkSheets: Psalms and Proverbs
What If...? 450 Thought-Provoking Questions to
    Get Teenagers Talking, Laughing, and Thinking
Would You Rather...? 465 Provocative Questions to
    Get Teenagers Talking
Have You Ever...? 450 Intriguing Questions
    Guaranteed to Get Teenagers Talking

Clip Art

ArtSource: Stark Raving Clip Art (print)
ArtSource CD-ROM: Ultimate Clip Art

Videos

EdgeTV
The Heart of Youth Ministry: A Morning with Mike
    Yaconelli
Next Time I Fall in Love Video Curriculum
Understanding Your Teenager Video Curriculum

Student Books

Grow For It Journal
Grow For It Journal through the Scriptures
What Would Jesus Do? Spiritual Challenge Journal
WWJD Spiritual Challenge Journal: The Next Level
Wild Truth Journal for Junior Highers

By Nikki